I0530337

**NEW EDITION**

# STANDING FOR GOD IN A PERVERSE GENERATION

REV. DR. CHRIS OKEKE

**STANDING FOR GOD IN A PERVERSE GENERATION**
Copyright © 2024 **Rev. Dr. Chris Okeke**

ISBN (Paperback): 978-1-964494-13-5
ISBN (Ebook): 978-1-964494-14-2

All rights reserved. No part of this book may be used or reproduced by any means, graphic, electronic, or mechanical, including photocopying, recording, taping or by information storage and retrieval system without the written permission of the author except in the case of brief quotations embodied in critical articles and reviews.

Because of the dynamic nature of the Internet, any web addresses or links contained in this book may have changed since publication and may no longer be valid. The views expressed in the work are solely those of the author and do not necessarily reflect the views of the publisher, and the publisher hereby disclaims any responsibility for them.

Printed in the United States of America.

**PROMINENT**
**BOOKS**
EDGE

5830 E 2nd St, Ste 7000 #9983
Casper, WY 82609
USA

# Contents

# Introduction

The ultimate intention of God is for His children to stand for Him in every area of worship, primarily in our Faith, Belief, Trust, Holy Living and in Obedience to His commandments.

Presently, we live in a perverse world. Our godly ethics of living are continually being adulterated as a way of sin. Sin is going against God's ordinances. The result of our sinful ways produces misery. There is sickness, disease, fear, death, wars and rumors of wars, there is uncertainty of life. Some unethical behaviors are noticeable among our children on a daily basis. Our enemy Satan seems to have intensified and updated his onslaught on humanity through luring unsuspecting children of God into believing and trusting things other than God, who called us through His son Jesus Christ. God is looking for that one who will stand for Him through Jesus Christ in the midst of these evil occurrences. Jesus said in the book of John, "The thief does not come except to steal, and to kill, and to destroy. I have come that they may have life, and that they may have it more abundantly." John 10:10.

We are equipped to stand against the wiles of the enemy. God wants us to stand in the victory Jesus won through Jesus Christ's sacrificial death at the cross and resurrection. Moses said to the Jews, stand still and see the salvation of the Lord.

As you go through this classic Christian book, the Holy Spirit who is my teacher will reveal to you the essence of standing for the Lord in this perverse and crooked generation. Are you ready to stand for God? If you are, God is extending His Grace for service. Paul, addressing his audience, the Ephesians, said, "Put on the whole armor of God, that you may be able to stand to against the schemes of the devil." Ephesians 6:11(ESV)

1

# Acknowledgement

The church is on a mission to reconcile the world to God. We are called and equipped to carry out this mission, yes you are called before the foundation of the world to stand for God. Jeremiah 1:5.

God is presently prompting you through whatever you are going through to stand for Him in this mandate until the world come to know Him through the salvation of their soul.

Are you standing for Him?

I will like to acknowledge men and women of God whom I would like to call "GOD's GENERALS" who stood for God in obedience and as a result we come to the knowledge of Jesus Christ through salvation of our souls.

I am grateful to my spiritual father, Teacher, Mentor Archbishop LeRoy Bailey Jr. whose teachings, prayers and encouragement brought out God's given potentials in me which led to the writing of this book. Sir, May the Lord continue to visit you with Spiritual increase and wisdom in Jesus Christ name. To my ministry partners in Nigeria, United States and other parts of the world who in a certain way inspired me through the word of knowledge or prophecy, Thank you, I pray God's abundance of Grace on you and may your name be found in the lamb's book of life in Jesus Christ name.

To my Wife Mrs. Helen Okeke, thank you for your encouragement, prayers, counseling and encouragement towards fulfilling the Lord's mandate. We started this journey together and because you stood solidly in faith, and prayed for me, God reached down to us and stimulate anointing that led to the writing of the book. May the lord continue to bless you in wisdom and understanding of who He is in Jesus Christ's name.

To my mother Mrs. Florence N Okeke who has gone home to the Lord. All the values you taught me has contributed immensely towards searching for the Lord. I remember your kindness, motivations and your love.

# CHAPTER 1

# Standing for God in a Perverse Generation

Sometime ago I had a conversation with my Christian brother, and our conversation centered on our faith in the Lord Jesus and how the Lord is moving us forward in the ministry. He said to me, "Chris, I am standing in what I heard from the Lord." He said that the Lord said to him, "BE FAITHFUL TO ME." This sentence from the Lord stuck with me; we are living in a strange period of our lives. The book of Peter described it as "perverse generation." Figuratively, it refers to something crooked, something different from what God originally intended it to be. You and I know that the whole world lies under the sway of the wicked one, Satan and his cohorts. Peter's appeal is still applicable in our generation, to be saved from the perverse generation. Through the Lord's mercy and grace we can be saved from our participation in the depravity of the of the perverse generation. God is the only one who can save us from this crooked and perverse generation. He is looking for that one who can be faithful. One who can trust Him. Are you the one?

# A CALL TO THE CHURCH TO STAND FOR GOD

The season of life before us is a time which calls for the church to stand for God in faith. Those who have not come to the knowledge of God through Jesus Christ need to seek Him diligently. We are in a time the Bible refers to as an "evil day." We do not need a prophet or a seer to inform us that the world is gradually drifting away from faith in God to different forms of Idol worship. This book is to stimulate your spirit into returning to the Lord. If we return to Him in repentance He will return to us, if we call on Him He will definitely answer us and bless us. God does not want us to accommodate these evil days in our lives, but to turn to Him and be saved. God, speaking through apostle Paul, said, "Put the whole armor of God that you may be able to withstand in the evil, and have done all to stand." Ephesians 6:13

The need to employ all of God's promises in our lives and stand for Him is now more urgent than at any other time. As long as the coming of the Lord tarries, hard times will continue but the question is who do we turn to. God? Self? or the world?

In this book we try to present those who have stood with the Lord in a time of difficulty and what they did to stand for Him. My hope is that these examples will help keep you occupied with your love for Him as you go through difficulty.

I pray that the Holy Spirit of God will give you insights and reveal more ways you can stand for Him in a difficult season of life.

There has never been a time in the history of the church where the necessity for the children of God to stand in total obedience to the commandments of God has been as tested as it is now. God continually encourages His children

1.  TO BELIEVE HIM. Luke 8:50, Romans 10:9, Acts 16:31
2.  TO HAVE FAITH IN HIM. James 2:26, Ephesians 2:8–9, Hebrews 11:1–13
3.  TO TRUST HIM. Proverbs 3:5–6
4.  TO OBEY HIM. Exodus 19:5
5.  TO UNDERSTAND HIM. 1 John 4:6–7
6.  TO WORSHIP HIM. John 4:23

7. TO CONFESS HIM AS THEIR LORD AND SAVIOR.
   Romans 10:9

There is so much evidence all around us, our family, our community and our world which suggests that the world is collapsing as a result of sin. We all are gradually drifting away and have continued to move further away from God. For this cause, diseases of diverse forms emerged (COVID, EBOLA, etc.), wars and rumors of wars, divorce, mysterious events and death, and other ugly behaviors. Debased minded people are emerging. There are so many other negative factors influencing our decision to obey God and keep all His commandments. First, a lot of people literally refused to invite Jesus Christ as their personal Lord and Savior. This disobedience seems to be the main reason sins are dominating our land. We have allowed the voices of technology, false teachers, false prophets, the New Age movement (targeting our youths) to slip into our churches and mellow the word of God to their own ignorance.

In so many congregations of children of God today, people choose the kind of lifestyle they want to live. You see, gays, lesbians and transgender lifestyles and their supporters speaking loudly to teach that these lifestyles are in no way sinful against God. They also encourage children and young adults to engage in the same trade as they are.

"Whoever has been born of God does not sin, for His seed remains in him; and he cannot sin because he has been born of God." 1 John 3:9

Again, Paul make this clearer in the book of Romans: "And even as they did not like to retain God in their knowledge, God gave them over to a debased mind, to those things which are not fitting." Romans 1:28

To stand for God, we all need to humble ourselves and turn away from wickedness. Then, He said, He will heal us and prosper us again, but we all have to be accountable for what we did and what we are doing.

God who sent His only begotten son Jesus Christ to die on the cross to save us from our sins, is concerned about our predicament. He does want us to die and end up in eternity in hell, but because of His love for us, He had a provision for our escape. He said, "If my people who are called by name will humble themselves and pray and seek my face and turn from their wicked ways, then I will hear from heaven, and forgive their sin and heal their land." 2 Chronicles 7:14

God thinks God of you and I, and the thing God wants for us is total surrender. To His Lordship, confess our sins and turn to Him. He is faithful to forgive us our sins and to cleanse us from all unrighteousness.

## GOD IS WITH YOU

In our catechism class when I was young, we were taught that God lives in heaven, so I grew up with the concept that God lives in heaven, and that is so true. In the process of time, however, through the Scripture, in His own time and opening up the Scripture to me through His indwelling Holy Spirit, I began the process of exegeting the Scripture, and I came to realize that God is everywhere and in our lives as well.

God wants His children to stand for Him in your everyday conduct. He wants children He can trust who will exhibit His awesome characteristics through which the world will come to the knowledge of our Lord and Savior Jesus Christ. In your everyday living you are actually with God, walking around with Him. He is with you as you drive, walk, in the grocery, in the gas station, everywhere you are. He is there to show His glory.

Dr. Myles Monroe in his sermon said, "Stand on God's words and it will change you." God's word will change you and your circumstances.

A songwriter Malcolm Cartwright sang a song on standing on God:

> "Let us stand on the rock, firmly stand on the rock,
> on the rock of Christ alone.
> If the strife we endure,
> Mid the throngs who surround the throng…"

God is our ultimate, He desired that His children run to Him in a time of affliction.

Psalm 121:1–2 says, "I will lift up mine eyes unto the hills from where cometh my help. My help cometh from the Lord which made heaven and the earth."

God never fails to take care of His children. His blessings are abundant every given day. His mercy over us never fails, they are new for everyone, the Scripture says, Great is His faithfulness.

There are six major categories of standing for the Lord, which I will table here for later discussion.

## FAITH

Faith is complete trust or confidence in someone or something. The Scripture defines faith as evidence of things, hoping for the appearance of things not seen.

Faith is the main key to obtaining the promises of God. We serve the Lord through faith in His risen Savior Jesus Christ. The Scripture said without faith it is impossible to please God, and John 1:18 said, "No one has ever seen God at any time. The only begotten Son, who is in the bosom of the Father, He has declared Him."

## IN A TIME OF CHAOS

The reason for the chaotic situation or troubles the world is presently going through is sin. Sin has eaten so deeply into the main fabric of our system that it is affecting our well-being. Man has looked for a solution right from the day Adam sinned, and his subsequent separation from God.

The solution is obedience to the principles of God as laid down in the Scripture, the Bible. Sin is a disease, it is a weapon through which Satan capitalized to get to humanity, it is a smooth well-constructed path for Satan to get to his host which is man. God said if only we can walk in His path we shall escape Satan's onslaught against humanity.

God knows the state of man. You see, God wants us to always use what He has given to us.- His word. Remember what He said to Moses, *use what you have* (emphasis is mine) You have all that it takes to stand for the Lord, and the tools are His word, as stated in one of His instructions by the apostle Paul in Ephesians, "Therefore, take up the whole armor of God that you may be able to withstand in the evil days and have done all to stand." Ephesians 6:13

The armor of God represents the action of defense we must take in our spiritual lives. The Scripture let us know that we are not fighting against flesh and blood but against principalities, against powers and against spiritual wickedness in the high places. It is important to understand the battle plan before we can attain the victory. Obviously, the victory has been won through the sacrifice Jesus Christ made at the Cross, we only have to access it, believing and accessing it through our faith.

We are living in a time the Bible calls "evil days." Evil days are seasons when something unusual disrupts the normal system of our lives, a time where evil occurrences seem to be acceptable in our society, a time when evil-motivated behaviors seem to dominate the good occurrences in our society. If you take a look around you, you will agree with me that we are living in a generation that is totally different from what God intended it to be. Someone trying to describe the present situation in our world said, "The world is pregnant and nobody knows what is coming out of it whether good or evil." Listen, beloved, the word of God has answers to these issues. As a result, Scripture encourages us strongly to watch and pray, in fact it says pray without season. Are you watching and praying? Do you pray without season?

One of the things you 'll discover is a conspicuous attitude towards the things of God.

## MEANING OF LIFE

Notably, so many people today are scouting around and searching for the meaning of life. In Christian commentary, life is everything in and about God. Solomon the wise son of David said, "obedience to God and keeping His commandments is what life is all about" (emphasis mine). In other words, to comprehend the meaning of life we have to see God as the source of life. We are troubled because we all have turned away from Him. Turning away from Him strategically means turning away from Life itself, and turning away from life means uncertainty and death faces you.

We have turned to fame, fashion, technology and other forms of inordinate materialism instead of turning to God. As already discussed, if we repent and confess our sin, He will return to us.

If your mind is not directed, not only to give our life but to focus on Him with every fiber of our being, then, ultimately we will be missing His blessings. Talking about Jesus, it is said in Hebrews 12:2, "looking unto Jesus Christ, the author and finisher of our faith."

Who is your hero? Who are you focusing on? Jesus Christ or other entities?

As we go through this life's challenges, God wants us to look unto Him not one time but all the time.

My preacher friend said some time ago that God is testing those who profess Jesus Christ as Lord and Savior to see if they are true believers and true followers of Jesus Christ. Are you a true follower of Jesus Christ as God intended you to be? Did Jesus Christ die for you on the Cross? Is He truly your personal Lord and Savior? Beloved, our faith is tested through hardship including all the anomalies we see daily in our personal lives and in our society. God has already equipped all His followers to stand for Him as these storms go by us. True faith in Jesus Christ always stands for God no matter what we are facing. During the Iraq war, I recall about 30 or more strong young people were tied hand and foot and were demanded by their captors to renounce their faith. They refused, saying that they would rather die instead of renouncing what they believe in. This is exactly what I meant by standing in your faith in the time of trials. Jesus wants His followers to stand gallantly in any form of trial.

What precipitated the situation the world is going through is the fact that our God given system of living or ethics of living has been disrupted, and as a result everyone lives and does what pleases him.

Whenever we keep God out of our lives we directly invite Satan to take over the affairs of our lives; we have all turned away from God to other things which stand against God's purposes or intentions for our lives. We are all living in the time of evil days as the Scripture puts it.

Jesus Christ already revealed this season in the Scripture, and He and gave the church what I call a "prescription" to overcome such occurrences.

Jesus said, "I have overcome the world." Yes, the victory over the devil at the Cross says it all, and such victory was handed over to us. For you to experience this victory you must believe on the person that brought the victory. His name is Jesus Christ.

## ENDURANCE

Endurance simply means being consistent in your assignment; persistence is part of Christian norms. It is one of the characteristics of a mature

Christian. In this topic we are discussing spiritual endurance. God expects us to endure while we trust and wait on Him to change the circumstances we might be going through at the time. Spiritual endurance simply means the power to stand in your faith during hardship, persecution and or stress.

"But those who will endure to the end shall be saved." Matthew 24:13

In other words, God is saying that those who keep obeying His commandments and trusting Him even in the midst of various types of challenges shall be saved. Are you one of those?

Again, James 1:12 puts it this way, "Blessed is the man who remains steadfast under trials, for when he has stood the test he will receive the crown of life which God promise those who love Him."

The world narrowly came out from Covid 19 disease which troubled the nations of the world causing the death of millions of people across the human race. As Covid 19 seems to slow down, another disease known as Monkey Pox showed up with devastating effects which has been recorded by the CENTER FOR DISEASE CONTROL (CDC) as another deadly disease and it can spread through contact with an infected person.

There are wars going on in various parts of the world such as Ukraine and Russia, other nations suffer economic problems such as Nigeria and other parts of Africa. Israel and the Middle East, South Korea and North Korea are presently flexing muscles against one another. Peace and other comforts of life are far to be fetched. But those who trust in the Lord have peace. It goes well. Jesus said in the book of John 20:21, "Peace I leave with you." The peace Jesus gives is all-time peace, even in times of chaos and in time confusion. One who truly trusts the Lord is a winner and victorious.

Inclusive are the devastating and inhumane attacks from terrorists. Worse still are unpresidential persecutions of Christians in many parts of the world, persecution that includes killing, burning of places of worship, kidnapping of Christians and displacing them from their ancestral homes and places of businesses to mention but a few.

The governments of our nations seem to be helpless or are not doing enough to root out these evils eating deep into the very fabric of our society.

God has one word for you and I, He gave the clue of existence from His word as recorded in Paul's letter to the Ephesians and quoted above. "Put on the whole armor of God" (emphasis is mine). Jesus Christ is and remains the focal point through whom we can survive in these critical times of our generation. The Scripture declares, "If my people who are called by my name shall humble themselves and pray and seek my ways, then I will hear from heaven and heal their land." 2 Chronicles 7:14

## IN THIS SEASON

A season is a temporal period which comes and goes. Seasons are not a permanent period in creation. Seasons come with different characteristics. The other day I was talking with my wife that we have less snow this year 2023 compared to last year 2022, which is a little aggressive with a sort of wild cold. 2023 snow season was mild with less cold.

The Scriptures said there is a season for everything, (emphasis mine), we all go through seasons of life, there is a time to be born and time to die, time to be young and time to be old, time to plant, time to harvest. A season is part of what God put in place during creation. Every season that shows up as we live has its own challenges, however, as already mentioned, the challenges in any seasons are temporal, which tell us that it comes and goes. Jesus Christ in one of His teachings said to His disciples, "These things I have spoken unto you that in me ye might have peace, In the world ye shall have tribulations but be of good cheer: I have overcome the world." John 16:33.

The above Scripture means that all the troubles we are going through at the moment or we will be going through in future are included in one of the problems Jesus Christ delt with and conquered its power over us. He accomplished this great victory through the victory at the Cross. Jesus had experienced more challenges than what we have experienced or what we are presently going through. At the time Jesus was being crucified, He vehemently assured His followers with these comforting words, "IT IS FINISHED."

Friend, you are delivered and set free from every ordinance that affects your life and the lives of your loved ones. Yes, you have the victory through the finished work of Jesus Christ on the Cross. You have the absolute right to enjoy the fullness of your life. God's intentions are for you to enjoy your relationship with Him.

As already discussed, every challenge we are going through has happened before we were born and has the potential to happen again, so therefore as Christians and as believers in Christ Jesus we focus on and trust in God to see us through all forms of challenges.

Sometimes our affliction may be a direct result of our disobedience to God's commandments, so God allows the affliction to bring us back to our faith in Him, in other words affliction becomes a schoolmaster to teach us in the way of obedience to God, through our total surrender to the power of His Spirit.

## NOTE ABOUT AFFLICTIONS

Affliction can come as a result of our disobedience to God's commandments, sometimes afflictions or challenges comes as a redirection to give God our ultimate attention when we are paying attention to other issues instead of God; if we are not giving our full attention to God then we are giving attention to other things and God does not approve. Therefore, He uses any means to draw our attention to Himself. Other issues that expose us to the affliction is sin, that is going against God laid down rules. In general the Scripture says any souls that sin shall die. Sin attracts spiritual and physical death. When we sin and refuse to repent according to God's direction, God's favor will depart from us, and we begin to experience serious consequences from our enemy. Again, when we sin we make our lives accessible to the attacks from Satan which carry serious consequences. In your affliction and other challenges of life, God is with you and still loves you dearly. The Scripture declares, "Many are the afflictions of righteousness but the Lord delivers him from them all." Psalm 34:19

We the followers of Jesus face hostility from the world who oppose the teachings of Christ, and persecution of on a day to day occurrence. Have you experienced any kind of persecution at any time in your Christian walk?

God will deliver you from every kind of affliction that befalls you. He is there for you 24/7. As you continue to stand for Him, He will take care of everything about you, He will fight your enemies both seen and unseen. He will provide for you and make sure that you are not in need.

"But he said to me, 'My grace is sufficient for you, for my power is made perfect in weakness.' Therefore I will boast all the more gladly of my weaknesses so that the power of Christ may rest upon me." 2 Corinthians 12:9

God desires that His children should be happy and joyful at all times. If you are a believer in Jesus Christ, and discovered that you are not always happy, one thing is possible. You may still be living in sin, or you haven't actually repented and given your life over to the Lord. Examine yourself, repent, and go to the Lord in prayer for His grace to follow you. God wants you to be honest with Him at all times. He loves you.

## ADAM'S ENCOUNTER WITH GOD

God said to Adam, "You are free to eat from any tree in the garden but you must not eat from the tree of knowledge of good and evil, for when you eat from it you will certainly die." This was the first test of man's obedience to God in which man failed and plunged humanity into calamity.

The instruction God gave to Adam was very clear and understood. There was no mention in the Scripture which signifies that Adam did not understand what God said. Adam's acceptance of Satan's antics shows how unserious he sees God. The same thing applies to us today. Our inattentiveness to what God says to us in His word allows the enemy to bind us with different afflictions. We can have a total victory in Christ if we pay close attention in the word of God and apply what He said in our lives.

Adam's simple act of disobedience threw humanity into the bondage of Satan's camp. Every disobedience to God's commandments gives Satan opportunity to lord over us, this is not what we want and that is not God wants for us as well. God loves us so much as the Scripture said in, John 3:16–17. "For God so loved the world that He gave His only begotten son Jesus Christ that whosoever believe that in Him should not perish but have everlasting life, that God did not send His son into the world to condemn the world but that the world through Him might be saved."

Jesus Christ went to the Cross for every battle buffeting our normal flow of living.

The scripture declares, "The eye never sees enough of seeing, you nor the ear its fill of hearing. What has been will be again, what has been done will be done again: there nothing new under the sun. Is there anything of which one can say, 'Look ! This is something new'?" Ecclesiastes 1:8b-10.

Beloved, the word of God from Genesis to Revelation is very clear on the instruction of how to live in the midst of challenging situations. The people who have lived before went through some sort of both personal and national challenges and overcame all of them. They trusted God all through the challenges and were delivered; who do you trust as you go through issues battling our existence? Part of our discussion in this book is to exalt the characters of these Godly people, what they did to earn God's favor, and how they stood for the things of God. God chose them as He chose us to glorify His name and be a light through which the world will know Him Before we go on into this discussion I would like you to note,

1. God loves you (John 3:16)
2. God chose you. (John 15:16)
3. To have eternal life. He wants someone that will fulfill His intentions for humanity.
4. God wants someone that will share His love with others who do not know Him.

God called you through Jesus Christ to be the light of the world. The devil in his entire work attempts in our daily living to make sins acceptable in our world. He tries very hard in his deception, he tries to educate the world to believe that you can trust Christ and at the same time live a sinful lifestyle. Everyone who believes in Christ and still competes with the world is deceived. He is in the claws of the enemy; the good news is that you can get out of it, yes you can because Jesus Christ already paid the price for you to be free. The scripture declares, "If the son of make you free, you are free indeed." John 3:36

Jesus said that you are free believe Jesus and walk in liberty according to the word of God.

## THE LIGHT OF THE WORLD

This is a phrase Jesus used to buttress Himself and His followers. Jesus Christ clearly stated that He is the light of the world, the entrance of the light into darkness drives away darkness so the people can see. Jesus said, "I am the light of the world; he that follows me shall not walk in darkness but shall have the light of life." Matthew 8:12

Those who still live according to the worldly standard will receive the life of God if they receive Jesus by faith into their life as Lord and Savior. The darkness of sin will see the glorious light of Jesus Christ for salvation and repentance.

Isaiah 9:2 says, "The people who walked in darkness have seen the light."

God chose you to stand in His righteousness; when other people are turning away to other gods and other interests you still stand in faith. As a child of the most high God, He requires you to stand in faith, trust, believe in all His characteristics in this season of life, in a time of sickness, and in pain, in a time of war and in a time of peace, in a time of lack and in a time of plenty, in whatever of season of life you find yourself, God wants you to depend on Him. His standard never changes or alters, He is still the same, He will walk with you step by step to make sure that your expected end is victorious, through it all, all glory will be ascribed to His name alone.

Friend, you are equipped and designed to accomplish His assignments by the power of His Spirit who indwells you. You are not alone in your spiritual journey. Jesus speaking to His disciples said, "Enter ye in at the straight gate: for wide is gate, and broad is the way that that leads to destruction and many there be which go in there. Because straight is the gate and narrow is the way which lead unto life and few there be that ride it." Matthew 7:13–14

The broad gate as Jesus Christ taught His disciples is the worldly pleasures, and so-called enjoying life without Christ, which generally refers to life without Christ. But the narrow gate refers to sufferings and persecutions Christians go through every day, and other challenges that impede your faith in the Lord Jesus Christ. The Scripture encourages us to focus on the Lord even in the midst of these impending situations. It says look unto Jesus Christ the author and finisher of our faith. Jesus wants to finish our heavenly race and finish well to earn eternal life in Him.

The Scripture says that you will be saved if you endure to the end. As a result of your faith in the risen Christ He indwells you by His Spirit to help you to walk in His love even in the midst difficult situations. We have no capabilities and power to live as He desired us to live, but through His Spirit we accomplish His desire for us.

God is not an intruder but ready at all times to show up in in your affairs as you continue to trust and depend on Him. He said that He never leave you nor forsake you.

Beloved, standing for God needs the totality of you. It needs uncompromised faith in Him. God wants you to be a bold child, He wants to reveal to you more of Himself, He wants to depend on you to accomplish His plans for the world. Yes, He wants you to be available for His use, if you are willing and obedient. God is no respecter of man, He is more than willing to use you to His glory. Amen.

## YOU ARE CALLED

God called everyone who professed Jesus Christ as Lord and Savior to stand out for Him in the midst of different forms of challenges.

The obvious reason that Jesus left heaven for you and I was to save us from our sins, and through Jesus Christ we can exhibit His awesome characteristics, which are;

- Righteousness.
- Holiness
- Truth
- Trust
- Obedience
- Love
- Peace
- Joy
- Compassion
- Grace
- Goodness
- and Worship.

These qualities are part of who God is, when you become born again by making Jesus Christ your personal Lord and Savior as the Bible says, God will release these awesome personalities inside of you through the power of His Spirit, that is why we commonly refer to one living such a sanctifying life and that such a person is born again. If you live in obedience and continue to live as Christ lived, you are seen as the image of Christ. You are endowed with His potential, you possess God-like characteristics. Yes, you are equipped and empowered with His power.

Have you recently got an inner witness of the Holy Spirit that you belong to God? The indwelling of the Holy Spirit makes you a different personality to the rest of the world because of His potential is seen in you, you are a new creation you now focus more on the Cross and the sacrificial act He did to save you and secure your eternal security.

Psalm 82:6 says, "I have called 'You are gods.'" The fact remains that we are already endowed with great potential through the power of the indwelling Holy Spirit. So not only did God sees us as His children but also His assistants as well. We have the power to change any situation that is contrary to our well-being. We have the power to heal, the power to set someone free from the enemy.

Another reason God chose you is to portray all God's characteristics in your daily orientations mentioned above, so that through you He will draw mankind to Himself for salvation. When you honor Him through His characteristics, surely God will bless you and your generation. You and I study the Bible which was written by those who chose to stand for God's purposes. Abraham is called the father of all nations because of his unadulterated and uncompromised faith in the Lord. One of the main goals of a true born again Christian is to daily ask God for uncompromised faith in Him. Do you have the same holy aspiration?

Part of our assignments as children of God is to let the world come to knowledge of our Savior Jesus Christ and be saved for eternity. The Scripture declares to, look unto Jesus, the author and finisher of our faith." Hebrews 12:2

The book of Psalms 103:3 says, "Blessed are they that keep judgement, and he that doeth righteousness at all times."

Standing for God is not a seasonal event, but a lifetime calling. Your lifestyle and mine should reflect that of Christ's life of love, holiness, compassion, mercy, faith and trust.

Is your lifestyle challenged by the Biblical standard laid down for everyone who trusts the Lord by faith in Him as Lord and Savior?

The indwelling Holy Spirit of God continually reveals to you and I who we are in the Lord, I mean spiritually, especially if we begin to drift off from our faith and belief. In every situation of finding that you are drifting from your faith it is important to retreat, evaluate your relationship with God, confess whatever issues you have before the Lord and move forward serving Him with all your heart.

When you stand for God in obedience, God will definitely stand for you in every area of life, God will fulfill in your life the promises He mentioned in the book of Isaiah 43 and in the book of Deuteronomy. God never fails.

## YOU ARE ANOINTED

As a child of God, oftentimes we forget that we need the anointing of the Holy Spirit in order to carry out all the responsibilities the Lord has assigned to us. The truth is that we cannot faithfully do the work of God with our own perspectives or strengths. One of the most important gifts of the Holy Spirit is the fear of God. So I must spend time in my prayer closet, I do ask the Lord to give me sufficient grace to fear Him, fear in this sense means submission, reverence, trust, obedience, and keeping His ordinances. All these formulas makes a whole man of God.

God is concerned about the way we carry out our assignments, yes, God evaluates our love for Him through our obedience. "If you love me keep my commandments and I will I will pray the father and He shall give you another comforter that He may abide with you forever." John 15:15

God relies on His chosen ones to stand for Him in our areas of calling, which is basically reaching out to the community with the love of Christ. Every true child of God is strategically positioned to represent Christ apologetically through which the world will have the opportunity of earning eternal life in Christ. It was for this ultimate reason that God sent the Holy Spirit to indwell His children to help in the area of their ministry of the word to the world.

You and I need the anointing of the Holy Spirit in our lives purposely for the assignments He entrusted upon us.

The anointing of the Holy Spirit is the endowment of power on a believer to be able to carry out God's assignments. Are you carrying out your own responsibilities?

Here are nine principal factors that can hinder your stand for the Lord.

1.  If you don't have a personal relationship with Jesus Christ.
2.  Lack of the Knowledge of who He is.
    (Knowledge is a theoretical or practical understanding of a subject. It is a fact that you acknowledge through interaction or education of a particular thing.)
3.  If you are still living in sin after you have made Jesus Christ your Lord and Savior.
4.  Lack of love for God.
5.  Disobedience to God's commandments.
    "If you love me, keep my commandments." John 14:15
    Lack of love for Jesus Christ will hinder our ability to stand for Him.
6.  Unforgiveness.
7.  Lack of fellowship with other faithful believers. Do not avoid the assembly corporate worship.
8.  Lack of genuine love for God.
9.  Not sharing the gospel or winning souls. God desires a genuine faith. He searches every heart to know those who love Him and those who play church. Do you love the Lord? If you do, then obey Him at all times. Obedience to the word of God is clear evidence of your love for Him. Jesus said to His listeners, if you love me keep my commandments. Commune with Him and pray without season.

The Bible declares to pray without season. Prayer is the strength of believers. A powerless church is one who does not pray. You do not want to be in that category people.

It attracts a blessing from God to carefully follow His order of things. His loved ones radically follow instructions, which results in obedience to His words.

Be a disciple who stands solidly for God in every circumstance and one who follows His order of things even if what He is saying does not make sense to you. You want to be a true disciple of Jesus Christ as explained earlier. A disciple is one who follows his master. Are you one the disciples of Jesus Christ? Do you follow Him? Specifically, God's intention for you is to be one of His disciples. God wants you to follow Him no matter the situation you are going through. God has got your back, beloved!

## CONFUSED MIND

Right before our eyes we are witnessing our world being crumpled into what I believe and described as a traumatic system of living or lifestyle. A new, strange way of adapting lifestyles completely unethical and strange to the principles of living specified by the Creator of the world.

Everyone both rich and poor has witnessed on a daily basis a dramatic occurrence of some sort of mental exaggeration among the majority of our population we interact with on a daily basis. One noticeable emotional outburst is anger and frustrations which seem to be making its way in our society, especially in our children including the young adults. Worst still, our leaders seem less concerned about the dangerous turn of events in our society, instead they took advantage of the confused state of things in our society to build an archaic system which further creates an atmosphere which will eventually theoretically enslave the people. People are angry and confused, the ethical system of living which points to moral laws established by God has been trampled upon and carpeted. What we see in this season is the government changing the Godly ordained morals of living to create a system which opposes God's ways and commandments. As already stated, some constituted governments of our nations add in their constitution a pattern of living which completely destroys the conscience of the people they are governing. This behavior has upended the nature of man which the Bible describes as "Wickedness." Our generation stubbornly turned their back on God and focused their worship and belief on created things. God called this Idolatry. Idolatry is the worship of someone or other things rather than God.

When we carefully evaluate our relationship with the Lord Jesus Christ, obviously we may find that in one way or the other we have ignorantly been disobedient to God's commandments, therefore the Scripture is right when it says that, "All have sinned and fall short of the glory of God." Romans 3:23.

First, we are to accept that we have sinned against our Holy God, according to the book of Romans. Our acceptance that we have sinned leads to repentance and confession of the sins. Then, invite Jesus Christ into your hearts as Lord and personal Savior. if you do this the Scripture says you will be saved. Your faith in the Lord Jesus Christ makes you a child of God and gives you access to eternal life in Christ Jesus. Can you do it now to be free from the consequences and devastating effects of sins? God is more than willing to set you free as the Scripture says.

## MAN'S CHOICE

After God created man, He allowed him to have a free will so he can make a choice of what He wants and what he does not. This is a very unique gift from the Almighty God. You and I are blessed with a free will, you can now make a choice of what you need without interference. You can make a choice of what you want, Life or death, good or bad, bondage or freedom, believe in God or not believe God. However, God desires that you and I will make the right choice in every situation we might face. He still wants to participate in our daily orientations. He is righteous, everything about Him is righteous. God desires that every form of our actions should be righteous.

In the book of Deuteronomy 30:19, God speaking through His servant Moses said, "I called Heaven and earth to witness against you today; I placed before you life and death, blessings and curses, choose life so that you and your children will live."

God knows the evil effect of wrong choices and so He tried to elucidate man on the free will so that man can make a right choice in every given event. Wrong choice of events started with Adam in the Garden of Eden, Adam made a bad choice by listening to Satan instead of listening to the voice of God. Adam was not ignorant of the specific instructions given to him by God in order to continue in God's special blessings. God said to him, "Of every tree of the garden thou may freely eat, but of the tree of knowledge of good and evil, thou shalt not eat of it for in the day that thou eatest thereof thou shall surely die." Genesis 2:16–17

Adam understood the simple clear instructions given to him by God. Do not eat that fruit. Satan always wants to counteract what God said to His children, he wants to negate the commanding voice of God. He worked on Adam's mind and consequently tricked Adam to believe his lies, asking "Has God said?" and as a result of Adam listening to Satan's suggestion, he chose to do what was suggested. If we know what God said in His word, it will be difficult for us to fall into Satan's deceits. Refuse to listen to Satan's suggestions, obey God in His word. God wants you to be well versed in Scripture. The Bible is very clear about this when it says, "Study to show thyself approved unto God, a workman that needed not to be ashamed, rightly dividing the word of truth." 2 Tim. 2:15

Our total emancipation depends on our relationship with the Lord and how much we know Him in His words. Jesus Christ is everything to us. With His name we can conquer any spiritual or physical wars directed at us.

## MAN'S HOPE

The coming of Jesus Christ and His ultimate sacrifice for humanity through His death and resurrection brought total emancipation of humanity. The Scripture said: "For God so loved the world that He sent His only begotten son Jesus Christ so that whoever believes in Him should not perish but have everlasting life." (John 3:16). We are the reason for the coming of Jesus Christ to the world.

It is important to note that God did not leave us nor forsake us as a result of the sin of Adam which plunged man into enmity with God, rather He loved us but hates the sins in us. The Scripture declared, "But God demonstrated His own love towards us in that while we are yet sinners Christ died for us." Romans 5:8

God loves us despite the way we live. He wants us to repent from our sinful ways and trust and turn to Him for the salvation of our Souls.

The only effective way to be saved or to participate in Jesus' death is to invite Him into our lives as personal Lord and Savior. If you do this, the Scripture says, you will be saved.

Choosing Jesus Christ to be your Lord and Savior is a personal choice, it is absolutely important to teach our children to make the right choice at all times. I had a co-worker who said to me that he doesn't care about the choices his children are making, it is up to them if they want to belong to

Christ. You have Christ, then you have the devil. In life, one has to make a choice to have faith in one or the other.

First, let your children know that every choice they make shapes their future, therefore train them to base the choices they make on God's principles. Pray for and with them and ask God for directions before every choice they want to make. God must be part of the equation of the future of your children. Pray for the choice of the college you want them to attend.

As already stated, God wants to be part of the choices we make on a daily basis, as such we must have a personal relationship with Him. We must include Him in our everyday orientations, but if we exclude Him, He will stay away and watch you. God is not an intruder. When you invite Him, He will surely come in and help you make a choice and stand with you to make sure that the choice you make comes out in a manner that will glorify His name. Consequently, choices we make can affect our future and the future of our children and the future generation, so it is absolutely important to commit every plan we have to God who knows the beginning and the end of everything.

Precisely every choice we make must have its rooting from the word of God. Unfortunately, in this season we have made choices that have devastating effects on our future and the future of our children and our loved ones.

CHAPTER 2

# **Perilous Times**

**2 TIMOTHY 3:1**

The Book of 2 Timothy, Chapter 3 sheds light on what to expect during perilous times. This perilous time is the evidence that the world is coming to an end. I believe we do not need extra explanation to believe that we are living in perilous times. Take a spiritual evaluation of what has been happening in the world. In addition to Covid 19 disease, of which the devastating effects will never be forgotten through generations, as the coming of Jesus Christ tarries.

Some people in our society see the situation we are going through as, I quote, "The end of the world is here." In Christian circles, however, the view is different, seeing the situation as a sign of the second coming of Jesus Christ. The turn of events signaled and points to the fulfillment of the biblical prophecies of the second coming of Jesus Christ.

Other sections of faith believe that the daily occurrence of diseases, death, poverty, and other chaotic situations are because there is sin in the land and as such God is allowing the generation to suffer the consequences of its sins.

What our generation is experiencing today has happened in the past and the simple biblical explanation to it is called "SIN." The Scripture clearly stated that all have sinned and fall short of the glory of God. Romans 3:23.

A definition of sin says, an immoral act considered to be a transgression of divine law. Additionally, there are other simple definitions of sin:

> Sin is not believing the existence of God.
> Sin is not having faith in Jesus Christ as your personal Lord
>     and Savior.
> Sin is when you tell a lie.
> Sin is when you disobey the commandments of God.

Our generation has quickly turned away from God and focused their attention on various other distractions, which is idolatry. An idol is anything that we give more attention to rather than God. Your money or job, children, wife or husband, etc. may be your idol. God commanded that we should put Him first in our lives and seek Him. The Scripture said, "You shall fear the Lord your God and serve Him and shall take oaths in His name." Deuteronomy 6:13

God is incomparable with any other name. The Scripture says our God is a jealous God. He wants us to give Him honor, glory and praise at all times for who He is. He is our Savior and our Deliverer.

The Scripture says, (God speaking), "I am the Lord your God, who brought you out of the land of Egypt out of the house of bondage. You shall have no other gods before me." Exodus 20:2–3

As already mentioned above, life without Jesus Christ in charge can have a feeling of emptiness, confusion, fear and uncertainty. Jesus Christ, speaking through Apostle John, (1 John 5:12) said, "He who has the son has life, He who does not have the son of God does not have life." We are spiritually dead without Christ. Our spiritual life is the Holy Spirit dwelling in us. This occurs when we make Jesus Christ our Lord and Savior. He automatically sends His Holy Spirit to live in us. His indwelling Spirit takes over residence in us and replicates Himself in us causing us to live like Christ. Paul, speaking to his audience in Colossae, said, "To them God has chosen to make known among the Gentiles the glorious riches of His mystery, which is Christ in you the hope of glory." Colossians 1:27

Life in Christ is a life guarantee for eternity in God. The word of God declares, the punishment for sin is death, spiritual and physical death, God hates the sin in us but still loves us. The ultimate solution to what our generation is experiencing today is "Repentance" and turning to Jesus Christ. The joy of the Lord occurs when He sees that He is part of your life.

## WICKED GENERATION
## (MATTHEW 16:4)

"A wicked and adulterous generation seeks after a sign, and no sign shall be given to it except the sign of the prophet Jonah."

From generation to generation man has been discrediting Jesus and His ministry. The ultimate question here is does it mean that these people have not been seeing or hearing about Jesus' miracles, how He made the blind see, the lame walk, raised the dead from dead, turned the water into wine and so many other miracles. The people asked Jesus for a sign before they could believe Him, Jesus knowing their tricks and the wickedness of their heart answered, according to Matthew 16:4, as written above.

Up until this day the world is still doubting the existence of God and the miracles He did. They even doubt the fact that Jesus Christ is the Son of God. As a result of the wickedness of their heart, the spirit of unbelief seems to be on the fast increase and has occupied the heart of the doubters. The world is systematically turning away from the truth.

Jesus Christ declared, "I am the way, the truth, and the life, no one comes to my father but by me." John 14:6

When we turn away from the truth, we are actually turning our back on God which is very disastrous for humanity.

The words of German physicist Albert Einstein still echo in our minds. He said, "The world is a dangerous place to live, not because of the evil therein but because of people who do not want to do something about it." Yes, they did not do anything about it because they do not know what to do about it. They in this sentence refers to each and every one of us. We have all sinned against the Almighty God and as a result could not access the presence and the glory of God. Sin blinds a sinner. God hates sin but loves the sinner. He is willing to save us and deliver us if we are willing. Are you willing to be saved and delivered from this disease called sin? The

Scripture said he who comes to Him (Jesus Christ), He does not cast away. You can do it now that you have this revelation on how to be saved. Follow the steps as written in this book. Confess, repent and ask Jesus Christ to come into your life and be your personal Lord and Savior. Study your Bible daily and pray. Serve Him with all your might.

## IMPEDIMENTS TO A TRUE WORSHIP

Dr Billy Graham, a world renowned evangelist said, "There is no love in the world like the love that God can give you; people are searching for the meaning of life, but often look in the wrong places."

Our world is characterized by a lack of the knowledge of God. The circumstances we have been through or we are going through have been an impediment to the knowledge of the Almighty God in our lives. As a result of these we have lost our consciousness and our faith in our living Savior, Jesus Christ.

We are all living with a desperate inner cry of who will deliver us from the calamity that has befallen us (the result of sin). We live in a world where people embrace unrighteousness and reject righteousness, living without hope and trust in our Savior, Jesus Christ, living a life that gravitates towards evil instead of good.

## LACK OF THE KNOWLEDGE OF GOD AND HIS EXISTENCE

The governments of our nations seized the advantage of the advancement of technology in our world and indoctrinated society with self-dependence instead of relying on God for our existence. As already stated, the Scripture said, "my people perish for lack of the knowledge of the truth of the word of God."

The present technological advancements are fast replacing our knowledge and faith in God. God allowed the advancement in technology in our world so we can use it to enhance our service to Him, but instead we turned the totality of our faith to technology—we trusted what God made instead of God Himself. "What a calamity!"

The online commentary I came across talks of the present technology: "We have become the idol people worship." Think of how many man hours we spend on our cell phones, iPad, and TV on a daily basis. Equate it with the number of man hours we spend studying and doing the things of God. God needs our attention at all times. How many hours do we give to the service of God in a twenty four hour period?

God has intended technological advancement to be tools for propagation of God and is calling for His people to repent from their sins. The word of God, the Holy Scriptures, declares, "My people are destroyed for lack of knowledge, because thou hast rejected knowledge, I will also reject thee as my priest, because you have ignored the law of your God I also will ignore your children." Hosea 4:6

The church in the present age is experiencing one of the worst periods in the history of the church. In one of his sermons Archbishop LeRoy Bailey, Jr., the senior pastor of the First Cathedral in Bloomfield, Connecticut, said, "We are living in a season of testing," a time he termed, "WHO'S WHO."

As our faith has been challenged, it is an appropriate time to stand and testify, though the situation I am passing through is tough, I will still trust the Lord and will still obey His commandments. God knows the challenges we face every day, He knows how the enemy plotted it, and how to prosecute it. He also has an escape plan for you. He is there for you and I so we can have life and to have it more abundantly.

He said you shall not die but live to glorify His name. In many places in the Bible He said do not be afraid or fear not.

Are you the one? When the Israelites were passing through a similar situation the book of Exodus reported that Moses called the assembly of the Israelites and cried out to the people and said, "who can stand on the Lord's side" come to me. The Scripture said the priest, the children of Aaron gathered to him (my emphasis).

Yes, beloved, our faith is being challenged and God is looking for people who can stand for Him in faith and in obedience to His word. The Scripture embraces us with examples of men and women of God who have stood solidly for the Lord in their own time and have gone to be with the Lord; this category of people is termed "God's generals."

In the Bible, Joshua said, "As for me and my house we will serve the Lord." This proclamation was made in a time when everyone in the country was either turning away from their faith in God, outrightly embracing atheism, or were being challenged by situations they could not handle. Maybe they have prayed and cried to the Lord for deliverance, and the answer is yet to come, so in the process of waiting they get frustrated and pulled out from their faith.

Are you being tormented by the common problems of life or are you being chased about by sicknesses and diseases? Listening to beloved Jesus Christ is the only answer to any kind of problems that bug us.

## GOD DELIGHTS IN YOU
## (ISAIAH 42:1)

"Behold my servant, whom I uphold; mine elect, in whom my Soul delighteth; I have put my Spirit upon him; he shall bring forth judgement to the Gentiles." Isaiah 42:1

Ultimately, God chose us for His glory, we did not choose Him first but He did and presented us before His Father in heaven. Jesus' sacrificial death gave humanity an open ticket to God Almighty. Yes, as already mentioned, Jesus is like a go-between for God and man. In other words, Jesus Christ is the way to God. The wisdom of man and the elites in our society could not determine any other way to God. John tried to shed more light on this awesome revelation and quoted that Jesus said, "I am the way, the truth, and the life, no one comes to the father but by me."

## YOUR RESPONSIBILITY

There is enormous responsibility assigned to the elect of God. The Greek word eklektos translates to elect, meaning "chosen" or "selected" for God's Divine purposes. First they are to show God's glory everywhere and anywhere they are. They are to be committed to taking care of God's Inheritance, which is people. The Scripture commanded the church to care of the poor, not only the poor but also the rich, tell them of God's love and mercy, give them the opportunity to earn the gift of eternal life in Christ

33

Jesus. Categorically the Scripture serves as ambassador for the Lord. If you are parading as a believer of Jesus Christ, it is absolutely important to know your responsibility as a vineyard worker for the sake of the Lord. You are called to stand for and propagate the gospel of Jesus Christ. You are to stand for the Lord to portray God's love and mercy to the lost world. You are living today to fulfill this awesome assignment.

Consequently, you are to reach out to the world with the gospel of peace which only God can give. In John 14:27 the Scripture declared, "Peace I leave with you, My peace I give to you; not as the world gives do I give to you. Let not your heart be troubled, neither let it be afraid." (KJV)

You and I have seen how the world is troubled with lack of peace, uncertainty of living, wars across the continents, diseases, disobedience of various categories, etc. There is generally a lack of peace, but you who are in the Lord are engulfed with the peace of God. In all circumstances a true child of God has Peace. Some time ago a guy in my workplace approached me and asked for my audience. He asked me why I'm so quiet and peaceful and very easygoing in my orientations. With a smile I responded and said, "God made a different in my life, I have Jesus as Lord and Savior." I used the opportunity to minister to him the salvation message, he told me that someone had already led him to receive Christ as Lord and personal Savior. Beloved, Christ in your life will mold you into His image. This is not the first time I was approached by someone about the way I carry myself. However, I do not try to leave on my own but Jesus Christ lives inside of me by His Spirit. How about you, are you sincerely living for Christ? Have you been approached by people around you to comment "he is Christ like"?

Jesus said, "I am the way, the truth and the life, nobody comes to the father but by me." John 14:6. Truth is a fact or a belief that is accepted. The Holy Spirit reveals to us the truth of what God said in His word. The way, Truth, Life and Love are the most significant characteristics of God:

> God is truth and truth is God.
> God is love and love is God.
> God is life and life is God.
> God is the way and the way is God.

God wants us to believe in Him on these four Characteristics. Yes, it is part of God that is essential in Christian living. To believe in God for who He is and walk in His character is one of the duties of the Holy Spirit to teach us the ways of the Lord and also help us to walk in His character or attributes. Character is being involved in the action of a story. Attribute is a quality of a thing. These two powerful adjectives stands in support for us to add actions to something that has a beautiful quality. People need to come to Jesus to save them. It is the church's responsibility to spread the good news of the quality of who God is.

As already discussed above, as discussed above, those who God called His children possess these beautiful qualities and character of God. To be a child of God first you must invite Jesus Christ into your life as Lord and Savior. The scripture declares, "But as many as received Him, to them gave He the power to become children of God, even to them that believe on His name." John 1:12

A true child of God is someone who has received Jesus Christ by faith into his/her life as personal Lord and Savior. When this is done God sees you as one of the elect of God. You are special to God. You become one of those whom God has chosen for salvation, the Scripture declares that they have been chosen before the foundation of the world to take care of God's inheritance. 2 Thessalonians 2:13

Apostle Paul speaking to his audience in Ephesus said, "According as he hath chosen us in him before the foundation of the world, that we should be holy and without blame before him in love." Ephesians 1:4

One of the reasons Jesus Christ went to the cross is to save and elect you as one of God's children. Jesus Christ is like a love letter from God to humanity.

Anyone who receives and believes in Him will be saved, in essence you will escape the eternal destruction in hell which is meant for the unsaved individuals. Eternity in hell is not your portion in Jesus' name. Now that you are still alive, it is important to receive God's offer of love in the person of Jesus Christ, He is the only way of escape from eternal abode in hell. Hell is a place reserved for the children of disobedience, who reject God's offer of salvation in His Son, Jesus Christ. If you answer God's call through Jesus Christ, then you will be enlisted as one of those elected to stand for the things of God. Your election becomes authentic right before the foundation of the world to be God's representatives in the world to those that have rejected Him as their Lord and personal Savior.

Receiving Jesus Christ into your life as Lord and Savior is the evidence that you have signed in to be one of God's elect. Christ in your life is the only significant evidence of your total surrender to His lordship and the will of God.

In further clarification, God's elect are those individuals who heard the word of God, believe Him, confess their sins and invite Jesus Christ into their life as personal Lord and Savior. (Romans 10:9)

Are you one of the elect of God? Have you signed Him in your heart? Does the Lamb's book of life contain your name as one of the elect? The Scripture further gave information about the elect of God. Their names are written in the Lamb's book of life according to the book of Revelation, "Anyone whose names are not written in the book of life was cast into the lake of fire." Revelation 20:15

If your name is not among the elect of God or if your name is not written in the book of life, then you have the opportunity to make Jesus Christ your personal Lord and personal Savior now in order to escape eternal death in hell fire. Will you do that?

## SALVATION PRAYER

This is a simple prayer offered to someone who wants to give his life over to the Lord. After the person who is intending to surrender his life to the Lord has understood why it is necessary for him to trust Jesus Christ as Lord and Savior, the scripture says, "For with the heart we believe unto justice but with the mouth confession is made unto salvation." Romans 10:10

The Salvation prayer is the most significant and important prayer one can say to become a believer of Jesus Christ. To break it down, start thus,

BELIEVE that you are a sinner. Romans 3:23

CONFESS your sins. John 1:9

REPENT from it;

ASK JESUS CHRIST to come into your life and be your personal Lord and savior. Romans 10:9

Thank Him from the bottom of your heart for saving you.

If you believe what you confessed, the Scripture says you will be saved.

Start to read and study your Bible every day.

Pray every day.

Join a church that studies and preaches from the Bible.

Jesus said unto him, "I am the way, the truth, and the life, no man cometh unto the father but by me. If you have known me you should have known my father also: and from henceforth ye know Him, and have seen Him." John 14:6–7

Salvation of our souls comes only through Jesus Christ, there is no other way. This true statement was what John was trying to explain and pass it on to us.

Note: our salvation is through the Grace of God, meaning that we did not earn it through any means, not our works or dedication to work but through Grace. We escape the tumult of hell fire through the salvation of our souls.

## THE BOOK OF LIFE

The book of life is God's record of the people who will live eternally with Him in heaven, obviously those who have made Jesus Christ their personal Lord and Savior are the names written in God's book of life. Listen to the word of God in Exodus 32:33: "Whoever has sinned against me, I will blot him out of my book."

All believers' names are written in God's book of life. Is your name written in God's book? If your name is in there, then you are part of God's elect. Alternatively, if your name is not in the book of life then you are not going to live with God eternally. Your faith in the Lord Jesus Christ alone qualifies you as one of the best candidates for heaven; yes, you will join the multitude of believers enroute to eternal life in God. If you have not given your life over to the Lord Jesus Christ do it now while you are still alive for today is the day of salvation the Scripture says. His grace is sufficiently available for you even now so you can become one of the elect of God.

The Scripture declares that you are elected before you were born. The book of Jeremiah explained it clearly this way, "Before I formed you in the womb I knew you, before you were born I set you apart; I appointed you as a prophet to the nations." Jeremiah 1:5

The scripture said that God has a plan for you and part of the plan is for you to fulfill your calling. You were born for a reason. Listen, beloved, you are not a mistake to humanity. God did not make a mistake sending you the world, therefore ask God to reveal to you the reason for living. God is interested in you, He loves you and wants to make sure that you succeed, and as such you should carry yourself with dignity as you look unto Jesus Christ. You are a child of destiny. Seek to find your purpose for life then you can freely flow spiritually in the presence of the Holy Spirit who will reveal all things to you. He will tell you why you are here and the assignments you are supposed to be engaged in. As already discussed, if you confess Jesus as Lord and Savior, He will equip you with all you need to be a successful Christian.

As a result of your confession of faith in Jesus Christ, God automatically releases His Spirit to indwell you and cause you to become a kingdom-minded child of God. All kingdom-minded children of God are the elect of God, their names are written in the book of life.

## GOD'S INTENTION FOR YOU

God's absolute intention for His elect has always been for them to stand for Him. Standing for God involves the totality of our being which includes the Spirit, Soul, and Body. God wants the overall being of mankind to stand in worship and adoration of Him. Every part of your being is anointed to carry out and fulfill God's desires. They must agree to praise God, when the word of said you are saved.

As we worship and adore Him, we are obviously responding to God's offer of love through His only begotten Son, Jesus Christ. The Scripture declared immensely that God loves us so much. (John 3:16) He desires our worship and adoration, He desires our connectivity through our worship and adoration. God gave us His Son, Jesus Christ, for the redemption of mankind. Redemption is the act of saving or being saved from sins, errors or evil (online definition). As already stated, God's absolute reality for us is to make us a new person like Himself, a person in Him who looks like and who is focused on humanity, you and I and the whole world. Yes, His purpose for you is demonstrated on the Cross of Calvary. The Cross is so significant that it continues to speak to the world from generation to generation. How about you? How do you see the Cross? Does it still minister to you?

## THE BLOOD OF JESUS CHRIST

God focuses His love on you, you are special to Him. He already planned your destiny in an extraordinary way. He demonstrated His love for you, He redeemed and positioned you for greatness.

You and I have been redeemed by the blood. You cannot talk about the blood without mentioning the Cross and you cannot talk about the Cross without mentioning the blood.

Redemption puts you in the category of a new person in Jesus Christ, or a born again person. You are like you have never sinned before, you are a new person. That is why the Bible calls you, "born again" after you have received Christ in your life as Lord and a personal Savior.

Jesus said to Nicodemus, a great Bible teacher, "you must be born again." We too, also must be born again (John 3:3), we must let Jesus rule our lives. As a confession of our faith in Jesus Christ we become righteous because He is righteous.

The Scripture also informed us that as many as receive Jesus in their life as Lord and Savior, God gave them the right to become the Sons God (John 1:12). Do you consider yourself a child of God? If you were to die, have you settled with the Lord that you will be with Him in heaven? Identifying with Christ is one of the primary reasons He called us. He stretched His Grace on you to the left you as one of His.

Jesus said, "I have come for the sinners and not the righteous." Jesus Christ is the epicenter of humanity, that is why the book of Hebrews clearly stated, "Looking unto Jesus Christ, the author and finisher of our faith." (Hebrews 12:2). In essence, Christ started with you and will end with you if we continue to trust Him.

## A TRUE CHRISTIAN

Oftentimes, people refer to someone who goes to church every Sunday and participates in all the church programs and activities and may even be one of the leaders, as a true Christian. It is not so, beloved; so who is a true

Christian? There are two distinct definitions of a Christian, first, Christian is one who professes Christianity or its teaching. Secondly, it is a person who receives Christian teaching or a person believing in Christianity.

Theologically in coordination of all the definitions, a true Christian is someone who has confessed Jesus Christ as personal Lord and Savior. The scripture refers to such a person as a "Born again Christian," born again because your old life of sin is gone, you now have a new life in Christ Jesus. As a result you have become a Christ follower and subsequently a disciple of Jesus Christ.

As a disciple, God has equipped you with His anointing to follow and obey His commandments.

As a Christ follower, God desires that you should stand for Him in obedience in all things as well as worship and adoration. Yes, you are chosen and spiritually packaged to stand for God in any given situation.

You are ambassadors for Christ. An ambassador is someone who represents or is a promoter of a specific activity in another sovereign country. You have a specific calling to represent and promote the gospel of our Lord and Savior Jesus Christ in this world. You are a defender or apologist of the gospel of Jesus Christ. Apologetics means, a defender of the truth of the gospel. Yes, you are to prove to the world the truth of the gospel and who Christ said He is - our Savior.

You must stand to defend your faith in the Lord and the gospel of our Lord Jesus Christ at all costs, starting with people around you and in the world at large until the world comes to the realization that there is no other name given among men by which man will be saved but the name of Jesus Christ.

## A GO-BETWEEN

A go-between is a word used to describe someone who stands between two people for certain purposes or in agreement. Jesus Christ stood between humanity and God the Father. According to the book of Genesis, God created man in His own image to worship or fellowship with Him. Adam and Eve's fellowship with God was perfect in the Garden of Eden, until sin crept in, causing a separation between God and man. As a result of His love, God willed in Himself to bring man back to Himself by sending Jesus Christ to die on the Cross in order to redeem you and I, and restore that fellowship mankind originally had with Him. Jesus died for this very reason.

We worship God through Jesus Christ. Jesus is like a go-between for God and man. He is the Savior of the world. God sees us in Jesus Christ. Apostle Paul explained it this way to the churches in Colossae, "For you died and your life is hidden with Christ in God." Colossians 3:3

"And you are Christ, and Christ is God's. 1 Corinthians 3:23

Jesus Christ is the Grace and mercy of God to humanity, He is the life we live. He is the exact image of the invisible God the Father. Jesus Christ is like a bridge through which man is accepted in God. We all have access to God through Jesus Christ.

As stated above, Jesus said to Nicodemus, "You must be born again." In other words, you must have the life of God in you for you are created in the image of God (Genesis). Therefore, you must possess a godly quality of living, not a worldly standard of living. You and I have lived a worldly lifestyle until Jesus came into our lives, transformed us and has continued the process of transformation into His image. Apostle Peter narrated it this way, "Blessed be the God and father of our Lord Jesus Christ, who according to His great mercy has caused us to be born again to a living hope through the resurrection of Jesus Christ from the dead." 1 Peter 1:3

## NEW LIFE IN JESUS CHRIST

Apostle Paul shed more light on this assertion when he said, "If anyone is in Christ, he is a new creation, old things have passed away, behold all things have become new." 2 Corinthians 5:17

Have you come to the realization that when Jesus Christ becomes your Lord and personal Savior, you are a new you or a new creation as Apostle Paul puts it? Your old lifestyle of sinful behaviors are replaced with the new life of righteous behavior. You now become uncomfortable with ways that are not Biblically orchestrated, you are totally transformed and redeemed into the image of Christ in God. You are endowed with the image and quality of God through Jesus Christ. Yes, that's who you are, a totally new way of reasoning and a new way of handling situations and circumstances that are clouding around you and your loved ones. A total new set of friends that will be a tool for spiritual growth and other forms of blessing. Most times I take time out to reflect on who I was before Jesus Christ came into my life and who I am today and I praise Him. Life in Christ is the best, pray to spend life in this side of eternity. In the time of adversity and chaos in our world and specifically our life, Christ gives us hope and comfort. You can always hear the still small voice saying, "I am with you and will never leave you nor forsake you." What a great hope! Therefore, beloved, strive to live for Him and In Him alone.

## THE CROSS OF JESUS CHRIST
## A PLACE OF EXCHANGE

Whenever I come across an object that looks like a cross, be it a cross made out of paper, or wood my mind usually races back to the Cross of Jesus Christ and what it stands for us as Christians. I have on a number of occasions come across someone wearing a cross on his neck, unconsciously I will feel some inner unexplainable feelings which disappear as soon as I walk away from the spot. Sometimes I will say, "I like your Cross," in a most unusual way and will initiate a conversation to know if the individual knows the significance of a cross he is wearing.

Basically, the Cross reminds every Christian about the death, burial and resurrection of our Lord and Savior Jesus Christ. It is a place where the final blow was unleashed against the enemy of humanity - Satan. It was a place where victory was achieved by the Lord Jesus Christ and power and authority given to all believers in the name of Jesus Christ.

Luke 9:1 says, "Then he called his twelve disciples together, and gave them power and authority over all devils, and to cure diseases."

Matthew 28:18–19 says, "And Jesus came and spoke to hem saying, All authority has been given to me in heaven and on the earth. Go therefore and make disciples of all nations baptizing them in the name of the father and of the son and of the Holy Spirit."

The Cross also reminds us that it is a place of exchange. Jesus Christ took our sins which originated from Adam, and which brought death, sickness, diseases and all forms of afflictions that befall humanity and nailed them to the Cross and in exchange gave humanity His righteousness and said to us, "go, it is finished."

How do you feel when you see a cross sign?

As a Christian, the Cross of Jesus speaks to our minds the episode or drama that Jesus Christ went through because you and I. A place He died as man, buried in the grave and rose from the dead as God according to the Scripture. The only way to experience the benefits of the Cross is to give your life over to the Lord. Have you done so?

## BEFORE YOU COME TO JESUS

In Christian circles you may obviously hear the term "born again." A born again person is one who has given his life over to the Lord Jesus Christ to be his or her personal Lord and Savior.

Another term is unbeliever, this category of persons speaks of someone who has not given his or her life over to the Lord. Before I become born again Christian some of the following habits were obvious in my life. How about you?

Can you remember the habits that you had been exhibiting before you invited Jesus Christ into your life as Lord and Savior? Some of the details of behavior you and I exhibited were;

- Criticizing servants of God
- Laziness
- Bearing false witnesses
- Disrespect to parents and adults
- Manipulations
- Drinking
- Lying
- Cheating
- Stealing
- Adultery
- Fornication
- Unforgiveness
- Complaining and bickering
- Bitterness
- Feeling unsatisfactory
- Antagonistic behavior towards the things of God and man

- Jealousy Failure to obey God's commandments and so many anti-Christ habits we exhibit in our lives
- Failure to recognize God as God
- Fear of the unknown
- Having a feeling of hopelessness when there is hope in God, etc.

## EVIDENCE OF A NEW LIFE IN CHRIST

When Jesus Christ takes up residence in your life the first thing that happens is: 1. Transformation:

Theologically, transformation means renewal or change of your life from the worldly kind of lifestyle to the lifestyle that pleases God. Apostle Paul said, "Therefore if any is in Christ he is a new creature old things are passed away behold all things have become new." 2 Corinthians 5:17

Transformation ushers in a new person in you. A totally new person that is ultimately different from the life you used to live, you will experience some sort of renewal in your spirit. You will think more of life and what it holds for you. Your attention will focus on what Christ did for you through the Cross. This experience will be continued day after day as a result of the fact that God released His spirit inside of you to help you live a life that definitely pleases God.

The outlined behaviors which you and I exhibited before the Holy Spirit took residence will be a thing of the past, you will no longer be coded together with those habits, rather people will be seeing the righteousness of Christ in your conduct, and in your everyday orientations. As a result of the indwelling presence of the Holy Spirit you are totally transformed to the image of Christ. (Born again)

As a result of a new personality in you, God sees you like you have never sinned before. His shed blood washed and covered you as you continue to live for Him. Jesus took all of them to the Cross and gave you in exchange His righteousness which includes peace, joy, and victory in all areas your living. All the problems including every form of affliction, negative behaviors, and sickness were nailed to the Cross. The Cross serves as a place of exchange, here God gave you His righteousness in exchange of your unrighteousness.

As a result of your newfound life in Christ you have become the central residence of the Spirit of God. You are not identified any longer as a sinner but a child of God. You are "Christ-like." You were not in the past, but you are in the present. If eventually you dabble into sin, God provides a way out. The Scripture said that you have an advocate with the Father. John explained it further in his Epistle, saying, "My little children, these things write I unto you, that ye sin not. And if any man sin, we have an advocate with the father, Jesus Christ the righteous, And He is the propitiation for our sins: and not for ours only, but sins of the whole world." I John 2:1–2

The former life of sin is gone, you are a new creature. As already stated, the characteristics you exhibited before you do not do exhibit again, rather you exhibit Christ-like behavior because you are now led by the Spirit of God to make sound godly decisions and not fleshly or worldly ones. The Holy Spirit of God speaks and decides for you. What a blessing to know that you and I are God carriers. He helps us to make righteous choices.

Apostle Paul concludes on this topic in the book of the Ephesians, "This I say therefore and testify in the Lord that you should no longer walk as the rest of the gentiles walk in futility of their mind having their understanding darkened being alienated from the life of God because of their ignorance that is in them because of the blindness of their heart." Ephesians 4:17–18

As you experience and enjoy the new life in Christ, the indwelling Spirit of God continually compels you to stand for God in all areas of obedience and in worship, adoration and thanksgiving. "Therefore, putting away lying, let each one of you speak truth with his neighbors for we are members of one another." Ephesians 4:25.

The joy of the Lord is your strength. Do you experience this joy?

CHAPTER 3

# Undivided Attention

This term means, paying attention to what someone is doing or concentrating on what someone is doing or saying. When we talk to our children about what is really important for their future, we demand undivided attention from them so they grasp what you are saying. Sometimes, God needs our full attention at all times, not only while we are in church but also while we are outside of church:

- In our homes
- In our offices
- Everywhere we are
- While driving
- While we are awake
- While we are sleeping

Everywhere and every time, He needs to hear your voice of worship and adoration. God wants you to bring your concerns to Him. He wants to meet your needs. God stands to be your only source of existence. He will do what no man/woman can do for you. Your destiny is in His hands. He wants our undivided attention. Are you giving God the attention that He desires of you? Probably the easiest way to put forward this question is, If Jesus Christ were to come today will He find you on duty, will He find you prepared for Him? Your duty remains what He commissioned you to do while He is away in heaven. Jesus Christ is coming back again according to the Scripture, so will He find you or I working for Him? Are you standing for Him in your calling, or are you waiting and looking at the other people to do it?

## ABUNDANT LIFE

Abundant life is one fully dedicated to the service of the Lord. It entails living in the fullness of joy, peace, strength for the Holy Spirit, soul and body.

Jesus wants all His children to live an abundant life. The book of John declares, "I have come that they may have life and that they may have it more abundantly." John 10:10

Abundant life is one of the promises which you receive when you make Jesus Christ your personal Lord and Savior. It is a life lived fully in the power of the Holy Spirit. It is a Christ-centered life (Colossians 2:10). It is eternal and rich in God's glory (Isaiah 43:7).

Beloved, when God promises a thing, He will make sure to bring it to accomplishment; has He ever said a thing and not fulfilled it? He stood by His word to keep you and I alive. He promises that we shall not die but live to glorify His name (Psalm 118:17). You are alive today because of His promise to keep you alive this year.

If you are not enjoying God's abundant life as Christ intended for you, then you are deprived of the most rewarding Christian experience.

### Factors that hinder abundant life:

1. Sin
2. Ignorant of who you are in the Lord
3. Partial commitment to your faith
4. Lack of commitment to the service of the Lord
5. Disobedience to the word of God
6. Ingratitude to God
7. Distractions
8. Other factors

All these factors and many others stand in your way of getting the awesome experience of abundant life. As already discussed, Jesus Christ came to deliver us from all the influences of the devil over our lives, these influences include all the hindrances that negatively interfere with our joy in the Lord and also deny us the abundance of life which God prepared for those who keep His commandments.

God strongly desires to and is abundantly able to deliver us from all these influences as mentioned above. He cares for us and does not want us to ever be separated from His presence.

## RE-EVALUATE YOUR LIFE

It is a good spiritual habit to constantly reevaluate your spiritual stand in the Lord. This means, pause, and take a look into your faith, believe, trust and confess of your faith In Him. Another obvious spiritual approach to re-evaluating your stand in the Lord is RETREAT, this refers to a situation where you temporarily suspend whatever you are doing to present yourself before the Lord to examine your stand with Him.

First, if we are sincerely serving the Lord, it will not be difficult for us to identify what is hindering us from enjoying the abundant life in Him. If sin seems to be the cause of your inability to experience the life of Christ (which in most cases is the problem), then confess your sins according to the pattern in 1 John 1:9, "That if we confess your sins He is faithful and just to forgive us our sin and cleanse us from all unrighteousness." Consequently, we must come to the realization that our sins have been dealt with when Jesus Christ went to the cross, so with this victory over our sins you can go ahead and enjoy your new life as a child of God looking unto Jesus Christ the author and finisher of our faith.

## GROWING IN THE KNOWLEDGE OF GOD

Knowledge of God means personal acquisition of who God is, His Deity personality, and His awesome characteristics. Knowing means having a personal or intimate knowledge of something or someone. In this context it means having a personal relationship with God through Jesus

Christ. Knowing or knowledge of God comes from studying the word of God and applying what you are studying in your personal daily living.

You must know God. Jesus said in one of His teachings, to Philip His disciple, "Have I been with you so long and yet you have not known mem Philip. He who has seen me has seen the father, so how can you say, Show us the father'?" John 14:9

Sincere service to the Lord comes from your knowledge of Him. In marketing, a salesperson cannot sell his products to his customers with first knowing the products so well in order to convincingly prove to the prospective buyers that the products will do what the salesperson said it will do.

God wants us to grow in the knowledge of Him. Your faith in the sacrificial death and resurrection of Jesus Christ qualifies you as one of the privileged children of God. When you trust the Lord, He restores the relationship and worship which was invariably lost at the Garden of Eden through Adam. Restoration of relationship with humanity was the ultimate reason for sending Jesus to the earth. Do you understand this? If you do, do you have a close relationship with Him? You can start a relationship with God by inviting His Son, Jesus Christ into your life as your personal Lord and Savior.

The first epistle of John further shed light on this when he said, "whoever has the son has life, whoever does not have the son does not have life." 1 (John 5:12). Do you believe that you have the life of God radiating in you? As already discussed, God indwells you by His Spirit who reveals the joy of the Lord, His strength and anointing for service.

## ONE-ON-ONE

It is important to teach and preach to the understanding of our various foundations of Christianity, that the salvation of our souls is based on an individual basis, yes, one-one-one account. Your loved ones cannot answer for you nor will you answer for anyone else. Salvation of our soul is personal, God gave everyone the opportunity to make that choice. That's why the scripture says that we should guide our salvation jealously.

When God called you in Christ, He meant you and not anyone else. He gives you responsibility and potential with which to take care of the responsibility while you wait for your time to depart this world. Moreover,

He indwells you by His spirit to help you live according to His instructions. Our overall worship of God is centered on Jesus Christ alone. We go to God through Jesus as already mentioned. Our communication and every approach to God is through Jesus Christ. Apostle Paul made it clearer when He quoted Jesus as saying, "I am the way, the truth and the life, no man comes to my father except through me (Jesus Christ). Hebrews 12:2

Jesus Christ is the only and remains the only way by which you and I can gain access to the throne of God. God designed us to always say yes to Jesus. A time is fast approaching when God will throw before our faces what we do with Jesus Christ. If you are placed in such a situation, what will you say to God?

Are you ready to give an answer to God concerning your relationship with His Son Jesus and your assigned responsibilities? Are you standing for God in your faith, belief, trust and obedience? Obviously, God will require you to give account of the responsibility He entrusted into your hands. Do you understand this concept? Do you know that there's no other way to navigate this than to accept the responsibility and trust God to see you through it. That you are alive means that there is something that remains in you which needs to be taken care of, some part of the responsibility that needs to be taken care of. A songwriter put it this way: "Trust and obey for there's no other way to be happy but trust and obey."

A lot of people in our churches these days are sitting and clutching on their chairs Sunday after Sunday without tackling their assigned responsibility. Basically, they know that they have an obligation to take care off, the Holy Spirit keeps reminding them that something is missing in their walk with the Lord, but, instead of them having counsel with the Holy Spirit, they seem to be shying away from it. I had someone who said to me some time ago, "I don't know my ministry." Obviously, he was trying to tell me that he didn't know what God assigned him to do. In the context of this, I advised him to pray over it, and that I believe that God will tell him what to do. Also, I said consider the scripture in 2 Corinthians 5:17.

## BE CONSISTENT IN HIS SERVICE

Jesus was consistent in His service to God and His service to humanity. He focused on doing and finishing what He came to do. He willingly surrendered to the Jews, He was accused of something He never did and was subsequently arrested, and was crucified on the Cross where He died for our sins. The Scripture further said He was buried, He stayed in the grave for three days and then rose again. Yes, His purpose by which He came to the world was to save us from our sins and give us eternal life. These were the things He focused on to achieve within a stipulated time He was given.

Do you know that you and I also have a stipulated time to live here for eternity? Within our timeframe God expects us to fulfill our assignments. Jesus knew what He came to do and focused on finishing it on time. Jesus completed His assignment at the age 33 years. Do you know what your assignment is? Whatever it is, God gave you the necessary tools to fulfill it.

Part of the plan of God unfolded when He sent His only begotten Son, Jesus Christ, to the world. Following this, Jesus recruited 12 people He named disciples whom He trained and commissioned to carry the good news of His salvation message to the rest of the world to save those who will believe. Jesus consistently reached out to the world with the good news of salvation, most people of the world heard the message and some got converted with the hope of eternal life.

## IN HIS ABSENCE

The parable of the talents in the book of Matthew 25 is the best illustration to explore what Jesus Christ expects of His children while He is away to His father in heaven. Listen, Jesus gave each and every one of us a gift (ministry) to be busy with until He comes back to the world, for us. The question is, what are you doing with your gifts at the moment? What you are currently doing with the gifts means a lot to Jesus.

According to the story in Matthew 25., He said a certain man traveling to far country, he called his servants and handed his business over to them. He have the first servant.

1. FIVE TALENTS
2. TWO TALENTS
3. ONE TALENT

Then he went for a journey. They were expected to continue with his business while he was away. In other words, he expected them to advance the business. On his return from the journey, not only was the business still to be functioning, but he expected to make a profit as well. When the man came back from the journey, he called the servants to give account of the talents he gave them to use while he was in a faraway country. The man rewarded his servants accordingly.

Jesus gave illustrations of what He wanted His disciples to be doing while He was away in heaven. It is essential to note that your calling is crystallized with responsibilities, these are your everyday guiding principles until He returns. Isaiah 1:19 says, "If you are willing and obedient, you shall eat the good of the land." God desires that you will be willing, obey, and stand for Him in whatever responsibilities He had entrusted into your hands.

Are you a Pastor? Pastor as if it's your last day on earth. Are you an Usher, Teacher, Evangelist, Counselor, Gospel Singer, etc., whatever it is that had God commissioned in your hand, do it and be consistent. Use the potentials you are blessed with for His service with such an intensity as if you were doing it for the last day of your life.

"But to each one of us grace was given according to the measure of Christ's gifts. Therefore, He says, When He ascended on high He led the captivity captive and gave gifts to men." Ephesians 4:7–8

The Bible confirms that you are endowed with these divine gifts. Living a life without exercising these gifts is like eating your dinner without knowing what kind of dinner you are eating, living without doing anything for the Lord is like living a life of emptiness, it is a life without a purpose, doing God's will refreshes you and gives you a rewarding feeling.

Your gifts are not meant for you to keep and go around it every now and then, it is meant for you to exegete the Scripture through which the world will come to know Jesus Christ as Lord and Savior.

You will be equipped with these gifts if you make Jesus Christ your Lord and personal Savior. Essentially, these gifts are part of the gifts of the Holy Spirit which are meant for the church. (You and me):

- Gift of healing
- Gift of prophecy

- Gift of discernment of spirit
- Gift of miracles
- Gift of diverse kinds of tongues
- Gift of faith in Him
- Gift of teaching and so on
- Gift of wisdom
- Understanding
- Knowledge
- Counseling

Are these part of what your life looks like? Have you discovered your own gift? Every gift which the Lord gave is for His service, the gift you have is not for show but to fulfill your ministry, your calling. You cannot go home to the Lord with them, consequently it is unwise to allow your gift to be buried in the cemetery.

Quoting from one of the greatest preachers and teachers of the gospel, Dr Myles Monroe who went to be with the Lord a couple of years ago, "The richest place on earth is the cemetery, there are untapped talents and gifts buried, beautiful songs that were not songs, mathematicians, scientists, engineers, great leaders that were buried with their great talents."

These individuals failed to use the gifts and potentials they were endowed with, so they died and were buried with it. How about you, are you going to be the next? Your gifts are meant for the living, you received instructions and knowledge from people who passed them over to you and I, so we have to do the same. Use them while you are still breathing. Go to the Giver of those gifts and He will reactivate and empower you to start using it. God will be happy if you do!

## IGNORANT OF WHO YOU ARE

Part of the problems we have as believers of Jesus Christ are the lack of knowledge of who we are in the Lord. Ignorant means lacking knowledge, information, or awareness about a particular thing, and knowledge means familiarity, awareness or understanding of someone or something. Knowledge or information about God is one of the prerequisites to proper obedience to God's commandments. If you do not know God, how can you obey Him? You cannot obey whom you do not know. Not only knowledge of Him, but you must love Him. Love for Him is seen in your obedience to His commandments. Your love for God starts the moment you make Jesus Christ your personal Lord and Savior according to Romans 10:9. When this is done, His spirit automatically dwells inside of you and takes over the affairs of your life including all forms of emotions for which love is one.

After one receives Jesus as Lord and Savior, the next ultimate thing is to study the Scriptures to acquaint yourself with who He is and receive the gifts of the Holy Spirit. Apostle Paul sheds more light on this when he said to his spiritual son, evangelist Timothy, "Study to show thyself approved unto God, a workman that needeth not to be ashamed, rightly dividing the word of truth." 2 Timothy 2:15

God expects His followers to pursue and discover Who He is. This is achieved through the study of the word of God in a consistent manner. As already stated, receiving Christ as Lord and Savior is the first step towards knowing who He is, then pursue the knowledge of Him by studying the Bible, the word of God. It gives you the firsthand information by the indwelling of the Holy Spirit, not only does He reveal Christ to us, but ourselves as well.

## WHAT GOD SAID ABOUT YOU

God said some wonderful things about you as written in the Bible. Until you discover what God said about you, you may not fully enjoy the awesomeness and glory of God. The Bible, the word of God from Genesis to revelation has a wealth of beautiful things God said concerning you. Enumerating all may likely take the pages of this book, however, I will point out some basic things God said concerning you as the Holy Spirit reveals them.

God said, He loves you. John 3:16

God said you are His child. John 1:12

God said that you are unique.

Do you believe all the things God said about you? If you do, then, you will have peace, you will not be fighting the people who are gossiping about you in your office or other places.

You are to have the assurance that Christ lives inside of you. It is only your knowledge of Him that will have adequate boldness to stand against every adversity that may come your way. Secondly, your knowledge of Him dispels ungodly characteristics or habits that inhibit your spiritual growth.

The Scripture says of us, "Put on the whole armor of God that you may be able to stand against the wiles of the devil, For we do not fight against flesh and blood but against principalities against powers against the rulers of the darkness of this age, against the spiritual host of wickedness in the heavenly places." Ephesians 6:12–13

The knowledge of the Lord also gives you access to do uncommon radical service for the love you have for Him. After we are born again, the first Bible class has always been to study the Bible daily and obey what it says. This is in order for us to acquaint ourselves with the knowledge of Him.

In our daily walk with the Lord we are encouraged to walk in synchronization of the Holy Spirit. One of His obvious assignments is to direct our walk with the Lord so as to live like Jesus Himself.

## THE ULTIMATE POSSIBILITIES ARE...

If you know who you are and what God has deposited inside of you, you will quickly begin to use them to the benefit of mankind. Your talent or gift is not meant for you but for other people. It's a gift that Jesus said hold and use it for humanity's sake until I come. There will be a time of accountability whereby we are to give an account of the talents we were given.

Are you ready to give an account of what the Lord gave you for the service of humanity? If Jesus should appear at this time or if you go to Him before He comes, are you ready for a glorious worship in His presence?

## SECOND COMING OF JESUS CHRIST

Have you come to realize that Jesus Christ will be coming back to the earth any moment from now? Are you ready?

## BIBLICAL SUPPORT

After the ascension of Jesus, the Scripture states that the disciples gathered together in one accord marveling over the news of the hour about Jesus Christ's ascension to heaven, of how men in white apparel stood before them and said, "This same Jesus, who was taken up from you into heaven, will come in like manner as you saw Him go into heaven." Acts 1:11b.

The episode created unusual events for the disciples, though they'd heard Jesus speak to them during His closed door meetings about the events that will happen (Matthew 24). The disciples were probably not happy that their leader Whom they depended on will be leaving for a different mission and they will obviously be on their own, they may also have doubted their ability to handle situations that may occur such as preaching the salvation message, healing miracles and other teachings that draw the people to the saving Grace of God. They had not yet built sufficient self-confidence and boldness to deal with difficult issues and as well as make difficult decisions. In sincerity, if we are to be placed in the same obligation as the disciples, we may probably be faced with the same kind of thoughts as they had. I believe Jesus discovered their fear and tried to encourage them thus;

Jesus said, "Nevertheless I tell you the truth, it is to your advantage that I go away for if I go away, it is better that I go away so that the comforter (the Holy Spirit) will come, if I do not go away the comforter will not come" (emphasis is mine). Beloved, you cannot defeat a situation until you face the situation. Moses in the book of Genesis never knew what Gid has for him until he made himself available for God's use. God said to Moses, "See I have made you like God before Pharaoh king of Egypt." We are to depend on the word of God if we are to be a good Christ follower. As we wait for the second coming of Jesus Christ it is our responsibility to do all that He commanded in His word. Timothy spoke in line to this assertion: "But you keep your head in all situations, endure hardship, do the work of an evangelist, discharge all the duties of your ministry." 2 Timothy 4:5

Doing the mind of God is our obligation and that is what matters as we live for Him. So it happened that as they were together, they saw Jesus ascending into the sky until He was covered with the cloud. The disciples were flabbergasted, it was an added experience, they had not completely overcome the experiences they had in the issues of diverse miracles they saw Jesus perform, and the issues of resurrection, now it baffled them seeing Jesus ascending to heaven until He was covered with the cloud. Some Christian schools of thought reasoned that the disciples opined that Jesus might drop somewhere in the bush so they could go and meet with Him. Others viewed that since Jesus already prepared them for the event of His departure to heaven they should leave and do what He commanded them to do.

While they stood ruminating on this occurrence and what should be their next line of action, the Scripture said that two men in white apparel stood by them and said, "Men of Galilee, why do you stand and gaze into heaven? The same Jesus who was taken away from you today will in like manner come again the same way He left." Acts 1:11

## MATTHEW 24:3, 14

Now as Jesus sat on the mount of Olives, the disciples came to Him privately, saying, "Tell us when will these things be? And what will be the sign of your coming and of the end of the age"?

Apparently, Jesus Christ responded to the questions posed to Him by His disciples in a manner that reveals His future intents including His death and resurrection. In essence, Jesus laid down some conditions that would precipitate His coming. In other words, Jesus' intentions must be fulfilled before He shows up. Some of the events are mentioned in the same chapter and verse.

- Wars and rumors of wars
- Deception
- Epidemics
- Earthquakes
- Famines
- Diseases
- Religious persecutions

Jesus used a parable in the book of Luke 10:12–13, to buttress further what the disciples should be doing in His absence. Jesus told them a story about a noble man who was going away to receive some honor in another country. The noble man called ten of his servants and gave them ten pounds each to do business until he returns.

Jesus called you as one of His chosen ones to stand for Him…

a.  In Belief
b.  In Faith
c.  In Trust
d.  In Obedience
e.  In Love

Jesus equipped you to stand for Him in all these principles areas. Belief, faith, trust and obedience are required with action attached to it. They are needed to be demonstrated.

As already stated, Jesus equipped you with all kinds of gifts and anointed you in other to meet the needs of His people. Our needs of Him varies from person to person. What do you want the Lord to do for you? What you expect the Lord to do for you is your need of Him. Apostle Paul in his teaching to the Philippians, stated, "That I may know Him and the power of His resurrection and the fellowship of His suffering being made conformable unto His death." Philippians 3:10.

Paul believes that he needed to know the Lord more and more. I believe that Paul's assertion speaks for all the people who have faith in our risen savior. Yes, knowing the Lord more should be the ultimate goal for all of us. The Bible is and remains the major source of informative outlet for who God is. 2 Timothy 2:15 declares, "Study to show thyself approved unto God a workman that needeth not to be ashamed, rightly dividing the word of truth."

Jesus Christ expects us to produce fruits and that our fruit should remain for the kingdom's purposes. The noble man expects a profit from the money he gave to his trusted workers. He wants accountability. Secondly, he wants them to be busy in his absence.

The rest of the story tells us that when the noble came back he called them one after another to give an account of the 10 pounds that he gave to each of them to invest in order to make profits or produce fruits.

This story is similar to what Jesus Christ did to the church. You are a child of God, God chose you before the foundation of the world, yes, you are a chosen vessel for God's purposes, you are chosen in Jesus, He gave a portion of what He wants you to do. He said, "OCCUPY TILL I COME."

We are invariably going to give account of our stewardship to him when He arrives the second time or if we go to meet Him in heaven.

We are to continue to stand for the Lord in the area of our calling, working diligently in His vineyard. You have all you need to be obedient in your assignments. In addition, He indwells us by His Spirit to aid us in our calling. You are not alone, Jesus is with us. Paul said in his book to the Jews, Hebrews 12:2, "Looking unto Jesus the author and finisher of our faith." We are to continue without wearing out, looking unto Jesus, meaning that we are to depend on Him as we continue to experience day by day challenges, distractions and persecution.

It is important to understand that the life you and I are living at the moment is not based on our achievements, it is not also based on a title or education, rather it is based on what Jesus Christ did on the Cross.

God wants you to hear His voice and strictly follow His commandments. Job described the voice of the Lord as a "thunder" and it rolls out of His mouth. And David in Psalms said, "The voice of the Lord is powerful, it is Majesty." You see, when God speaks He wants us to receive it immediately. He revealed to you through His Spirit, He speaks clearly so you can understand what He is saying.

He wants our undivided attention at all times, if you give God your attention He will reveal to you His awesome personality. One of the notable stories in the Bible was when Moses gave God his attention, then God revealed to Moses one of His names: "I am that I am." He also revealed to Moses His intentions for the languishing children of Israel in Egypt. He said, "I have surely seen the oppression of my people who are in Egypt, and have heard their cry because of their taskmasters, for I know their sorrows, so I have come down to deliver them." Exodus 3:7.

Moses chose to stand for God, as will be further discussed in the preceding chapters in this book.

God desires your total submission to His authority. We cannot be physically present and spiritually absent as we serve the Lord. All parts of our being must be involved and respond to the Lord's call to bless you. If God sent His Angel with a package of blessings to you, will He find you in place, will He see you? Or is He going to see someone else?

The only time you will discover your spiritual potential is when you choose to stand for God and follow His ways. In other words, you agree to God's terms of service not your own terms or ideas.

# CHAPTER 4

# Champions for Jesus Christ

To be a champion for Jesus Christ starts when you surrender your life to Him as your Lord and personal Savior according to Romans 10:9

"That if you confess with your mouth the Lord Jesus Christ and believe in your heart that God hath raised Him from the dead thou will be saved."

Those who heard the Lord's call on their life and answer, and obey what He tells you, are those that love Him and stand for Him in all ramifications, no matter the challenges they go through or are going through, and still stand in Faith, in believing, and in Trusting are the champions for the Lord. They are the children of destiny. They are fearless and are as bold as a lion.

These are the ones who can declare a thing and it will be established and the light of God shall shine on their ways. These are true champions. They operate under the anointing of the Holy Spirit. They hear the word of God and are determined to obey the command according to God's directions, not their own way. Joshua knew the important of standing for the Lord and made this declaration to his audience; "And if it seems evil to you to serve the Lord, choose for yourselves this day whom you will serve, weather the gods whom your fathers served that were on the other side of the River, or the gods of the Amorites, in whose lands you dwell, But as for me and my house, we will serve the Lord." Joshua 24:15

You can be one of God's champions if you determine in your heart to obey His commands. A lot of our beloved Christian brothers and sisters do not understand what it means to stand for God, some do like to stand for God in prayer. This means that they become someone who prays at all times, not just praying for your family but for other people as well, he will pray in any situation, during a time of war or a time of peace. He opens up an interesting communication with God through prayers and supplication. He talks to God of his needs and God responds by meeting those needs. God assures His children through Prophet Isaiah that if you pray He will answer you. "Before they call I will answer, while they are still speaking I will hear." Isaiah 65:24.

That means the answer to your prayer has been pre-packed and for you to take delivery of it. If there are people to pray, then there is a God to answer. Amen.

## TWO IMPORTANT QUALITIES

I had the opportunity to speak at an evangelism seminar organized by Rev. Anthony Iwono, the senior pastor of faith outreach ministry Rochester, New York. The church chose to stand for God through their obedience in winning souls for the kingdom of God. The seminar basically centered on how to be an effective soul winner. Some of the participants are fine born again Christians but still lack enthusiasm in soul winning.

They had all the qualifications needed to be effective in bringing people to Christ. It is not that God did not equip them but they somehow believed what the enemy is telling them and so they did not trust God's promise that He will be with them as they witness to the unbelievers. Now do you trust God enough to use you in the area of evangelism? After you are born again there are two major factors which God is looking for,

1.  WILLING HEART or determination, decide anyhow to obey what God said in His word.

2.  VAILABILITY. You are to make yourself available for the Holy Spirit for the assignment.

These two qualities are what God is looking for in your life as His child. Do you have this "willing heart" or "determination" in your heart to stand for God in the area of your calling? If you are willing, are you available for duty. If the Lord comes today, will He found you at your duty post?

To stand for God is Now! Believers are given the responsibility to stand for God. We are mandated to carry out these responsibilities. We are to stand for God in;

1.  Love
2.  Faith
3.  Trust
4.  Prayer
5.  Obedience

The absolute reason you and I are called and chosen by God is for us to serve as a vessel through which God's gospel of love will be preached all over the world, the grace of God covers you as you go to preach this gospel. Grace is unmerited favor. Apostle Paul declared to his audience, "For by Grace you have been saved through faith, and not of yourselves, it is the gift of God." Ephesians 2:8.

These five principal elements as illuminated above are essentials to standing for God, in addition, you chose to stand for Him, not because He healed, or delivered you or saved, but because you loved Him. You must allow the Holy Spirit to illuminate you with God's love so you can love Him; remember that God first loved us and demonstrated His love for us all when, while we were still sinners Christ died for us. Romans 5:8.

To stand for Him, our faith must be involved. We cannot love God if we don't believe that He exists. We also must trust Him for what He said He is.

We must obey. God values our obedience. In fact, God determined our love for Him through our obedience. "If you love me, keep my commandment," the scripture says. As already mentioned above, these four elements must be held strongly in our emotions as we stand for the Lord. We must pray that God will equip us on a daily basis so we can maintain and keep our stand in the Lord.

## WHEN YOU CHOOSE TO STAND FOR GOD

Your election to the camp of God is not what started when you give your life over to the Lord Jesus Christ. It did not start when you were born or when you started going to the church; no, not at all. It started before you were born, yes before the foundation of the earth. Jesus put a mark of ownership on you as a chosen vessel. A vessel is a type of container which can be used to hold a liquid or transfer such liquid to another vessel or a container. God equipped you with His anointing to be a vessel through which He will deliver His message or instructions to His people. Prophet Jeremiah said, "Before I formed you in the womb I knew you; Before you were born I sanctified you; I ordained you the prophet of the nations." Jeremiah 1:5

By reason of what God said concerning you through the book of Jeremiah, your responsibility should always be to focus all your attention on Him to discover what your responsibilities are or what your assignment is.

First, your primary calling is to have a personal relationship with Jesus Christ, and stick with Him, and as we continue in fellowship He will definitely X-ray to us through the inner witness of the Holy Spirit. What He will have us do, may be to relocate to a different country or community. it could be anywhere. When I repented by receiving Jesus into my life as Lord and personal Savior, then I remembered I asked the Lord what He wanted me to do, and He responded through the winning witness of the Holy Spirit: "WAIT UNTIL I TELL YOU WHAT TO DO." This was in Nigeria. I continued in the area of my calling which is evangelism. I and my team continued until we relocated to the United States of America, where I continue to share the gospel as I was doing earlier. For you, I don't know your work with the Lord nor can tell I you that God has a particular calling on you, but you can simply ask Him to reveal to you what He will have you do. That is why the book of Hebrews 12:2a encourages us to, "look unto Jesus Christ, the author and finisher of our faith who for the sake of the joy that was set before him endured affliction."

Yes, to stand for the Lord in holiness as we carry out our given responsibilities, the military circle says it this way: "no retreat, no surrender until the mission is accomplished." For Christians, we are to continue in the specific area of calling until we are called home to the Lord. Are you standing in the area of your calling? If your answer is no, then you have a chance now to repent and ask for the Grace of God to resume your responsibility for which you are living.

## THERE ARE 7 BIBLICAL REFERENCES FOR STANDING

1.  Faith—Watch ye, stand in the faith, acquit yourselves like men, be strong. 1 Corinthians 16:13. (KJV)
2.  For I know that my redeemer liveth, and that he shall stand at the latter day upon the earth. Job 19:25
3.  There are many devices in a man's heart, nevertheless it is the counsel of the lord that shall stand. Proverbs 19:21
4.  Wherefore take upon you the whole armor of God that ye may be able to withstand evil, and having done all, to stand. Ephesians 6:13
5.  My soul thirsteth for God, for the living God, when shall I come and appear before God. Psalm 42:2
6.  And when ye stand praying, forgive, if ye have ought against any; that your father also which is in heaven may forgive you your trespasses. Mark 11:25
7.  Blessed is the man that walketh not in the counsel of the ungodly nor standeth in the way of sinners, nor sit that in the seat of the scornful. Psalm 1:1

One of the obvious expectations of God from you after you have confessed Him as Lord and Savior is to stand victoriously and grow spiritually. For you to grow as God intended you requires absolute faith in Him. As you decide to grow in Him, the enemy of your faith will show up to make sure you did not reach your potential.

It was for the same reason of standing for God in obedience that Apostle Paul wrote to the Ephesians, "Therefore put on the whole armor of God that you may be able to stand against the wiles of the devil." Ephesians 6:11

"Wiles of the devil" in this context means, the tricks, manipulation or antics designed to hinder and deceive the followers of Jesus Christ from fully carrying out our main responsibilities. Therefore, friend, He who is omnipresent and omnipresent, reveals to us ways through which we can stand in the victory He won at the cross and stand for Him without hinderance. Jesus said put on the whole amour of God. The whole armor is the only weapon that can fortify you against the enemy's antics. If you do not put on the whole armor, you will become a prey to be devoured. God did not instruct us to put on half or quarter armor but the whole armor. God does not want His beloved children to obey part of His word, or to obey some of His word, but everything.

The armor of God is His words. It is only through His word that we can have victory over the enemy's antics. God said to Moses when the Children of Israel were about to cross the Red Sea, the ocean was in their way, Moses was scared but when he consulted God, He said use what you have. Moses stretched his hands, pointing the staff the ocean, and the ocean divided in two, the Children of Israel were able to pass and continued with their journey to the Promised Land.

What the church has now is the word of God, and when we stand in what God said, victory is achieved. Amen.

As we proceed in this discussion, we will look into this armor which the Lord wants us to put on. I want you to understand that you are the number one enemy of Satan. You see, after you have pronounced Jesus the Lord of your life, Satan (devil) hates you; he hates you because of the decision you made to follow Jesus. If he could have his way, he would terminate your life instantly, but God has the hedge of protection which the Lord Jesus Christ put around you after He chose you, and Satan finds it impossible to reach you or pull you back into the sinful lifestyle from which you were delivered.

The ultimate problem of mankind is sin. Yes, sin. We have all sinned and fall short of the glory of God. All the ugly situations, including sickness, wars, bad economy of a country, bad governance, marital problems, and family problems are as a result of sins. You and I may not have committed a particular sin, but the sin we carry from Adam is still active until one repents and confesses Jesus Christ as personal Lord and Savior—only then are we delivered and set from it.

The afflictions or challenges we go through on a daily basis are all orchestrated by Satan. Afflictions are the things that cause pain, distress, or suffering through physical infirmity, and it interferes with our sense of reasoning or judgement.

All the saints that have lived before us experienced the same or even more challenges than we have today. Every affliction or challenge is like a torment to our lives, buffeting us and interfering with our peaceful existence. But we thank God through Jesus Christ who set us free from every form of affliction or challenges. He went to the cross just to set us free from the bondage of sin.

So when sickness, poverty, death, and other forms of affliction begin to torment us, then the Lord Jesus Christ expects us to do one thing, that is to stand for Him, period! You stand for him as we earlier said, stand in believing that what He said concerning the situation, He will bring it to pass. Then you have to stand in Faith, and Faith is our complete trust in God.

The intention of God for you and I is to stand for Him: believing in Him, John 6:47, John 6:35 trusting in Him (Proverbs 3:5) as we go through various forms of afflictions and trials, more so, working in the vineyard where we were called.

Satan masterminds every form of affliction we go through on a daily basis, no matter the significance of the particular affliction. His ultimate aim is to discourage us from our faith in God, he hates you especially if you are a child of God, he wants you to cease existing, he wants to make your life unbearable. The book of John reminded us that Satan came but to kill, steal and destroy. Jesus said, "But I come that they may have life and that you may have it more abundantly." John 10:10

## THE LIFE OF A BELIEVER IN CHRIST

The life of every true Christian can be equated with a constant spiritual battle which does not stop until we return to God. Also, the life of a true Christian is marked with the joy of the Lord if we have eternal life in Him.

Every day, we live in a form of battle which we do not anticipate. These forms of battle start in the negative ministrations from Satan. He goes ahead to lie to our mind to do certain things which are outside of God's plan for us, as he places such negative thoughts in our mind, he follows it up for us to practice it causing us to sin against God.

No wonder the apostle Paul encouraged the Romans, "Therefore I urge you, brothers, in view of God's mercy offer your bodies as a living sacrifice holy and pleasing to God, this is your spiritual act of worship. Do not conform any longer to the pattern of this world, but be transformed by the renewing of your mind that you may prove what is that good and acceptable and perfect will of perfect will of God." Romans 12:1–2

This verse outlines some basic facts that for one to stand for the Lord does not require your physical strength or ideology, but your complete trust and alignment with the Holy Spirit. The Holy Spirit gives you the anointing needed for unadulterated obedience to God's commandments; yes, you need to align with Him. The work of the Holy Spirit can never be over emphasized when it comes to standing for God. Moreso, the Holy Spirit reveals to you the mind of God and what He requires of you. He reveals to you the armor of God and teaches you how to use it. These defensive mechanisms, Apostle Paul called armor, "the whole ARMOR OF GOD."

Apostle Paul, speaking to the Ephesians, however, gave further interesting narrative of what God meant by the whole amor of God:

> "Therefore put on the whole armor of God that you may be able to stand against the wiles of the devil."

And having done all, to stand, stand therefore having guidance girded your waist with the truth. Having girded the breastplate of righteousness. The armor in the Bible is a metaphor which is used to describe to us what they needed in order to stand solidly for God and the things of God. When persecution and other injustice are meted out against your faith in the Lord, you continued to stand in your faith proving to the persecutors the reality of the existence of God. The enemy launches his demonic missiles on a Christian on a daily basis. 1 Peter 5:8 said, "Be sober, be vigilant because your adversary, the devil prowls like a wounded lion looking for whom he may devour." Verse 9 added, "Resist him steadfast in the Faith, knowing that the same suffering are experienced by your brotherhood in the world." 1 Peter 5:8

Satan dispatches his demonic angels to fight against God's people. Not only does he attack people spiritually but also physically. In every attack of the enemy on us or on our family God wants us to stand for Him in His word and apply our belief, faith and trust in what He said. It is only on this principle of approach thar our breakthrough comes.

## 5 COMMON PRINCIPLES OF STANDING FOR GOD

Standing for God is one of the obvious decisions one makes when one receives Jesus Christ in his/her life as Lord and personal Savior. God does not force anyone to stand for Him; rather He gives you the principles which if you follow will bring spiritual increase which presents you before Him as an "obedient child." Also, if you obey and follow the principles, God will trust you and use you to accomplish His plan for humanity. The 5 common principles are;

1.  Believe in Him
2.  Trust Him
3.  Obey Him
4.  Have Faith in Him
5.  Love Him

These 5 principles will be elaborated on a clearer scale as we move forward in our discussion of standing for God. However, needless to say that these responsibilities, if obeyed, carry viable levels of God's parallel rewards for you and your loved ones. If you choose to stand for the Lord, He will stand with you and will never leave you by yourself.

Quoting from one of the Christian book expositor series by Dr. J. Vernon McGee, "God will point the way for you to walk, the way that pleases Him."

Obviously you are packaged, anointed, and ordained before you were born to participate in the kingdom building. Your primary responsibility is to create awareness and lead people to the saving Grace of Christ. Jesus

Christ speaking through the book of John to Nicodemus, "You must be born again." Nicodemus was delivered from religiosity to the salvation and Knowledge of Christ.

God spoke through prophet Jeremiah: "Before you were formed in the womb I knew you, Before you were born I set you apart; I appointed you as a prophet to the nations." Jeremiah 1:5

If you become aware of whom you are in the Lord and what God has already deposited in you for His purposes, and to stand for Him, your life will be completely transformed. Listen, you are a child of God and He has already equipped and positioned your to stand for God!

God is interested in you, He is interested in me, too. Probably that is why you and I are still alive and well. Being aware of this truth, it becomes absolutely important to immerse your life in the Lord believing and trusting Him in all things. Every Christian face different kinds of challenges confronting them, or things that are derailing them spiritually and impeding their clear vision of who the Lord is, candidly, those things that seemed to be distressing you are the tool to catapult you to the level the Lord wants you to be spiritually. In Jesus Christ's kingdom, the way up is down. Standing for Jesus Christ and His kingdom is a sign of submission to the Almighty God.

No matter the circumstances surrounding you, have faith, believe, trust, and obey is your watchword in serving the Lord. Other people including your loved ones may turn their back on you, and heaven may be silent to your needs, but God still expects you to stand in faith trusting Him to do something over such situations for which you are going through. God never fails to keep His promises. He said, His promises are yea and Amen.

## JOB STOOD FOR GOD

When Job was going through some horrible situations in his life, these situations included,

> the death of all his children,
> his friends left him,
> his wealth was gone,
> his wife offered no support,

STANDING FOR GOD IN A PERVERSE GENERATION

his health was in a sorry situation.

The only option left for Job was to die.

In these circumstances surrounding Job, he still trusted God and stood in obedience, Job still trusts God for a latter rain of deliverance and restoration. Job said, "Though He may slay me I will trust Him." Job 13:15

Job knew that his pain was not permanent and that God would surely restore him again. Job had unshakable faith in God, this made him to stand believing and waiting for God's timetable to fulfill His promise. The Grace of God was all sufficient for Job, and so he was able to stand solidly for God as he passed through this terrible situation.

Job stands as a solid role model for you and I today, that no circumstances can sway us away from standing and believing in God's words. If you decide to stand for God when situations arise in your life, God's grace will envelop and keep you until it is over. God never leaves anyone who looks unto Him for help. Listen, God will fight for you, He will disgrace your enemies, He will choose you.

## 11 CHARACTERISTICS OF ONE WHO IS STANDING FOR GOD

1. You must be born again
2. You must be a disciple of Jesus Christ
3. You must love God
4. You must be courageous
5. You must keep God's commandments
6. You must love the things of God
7. You must fellowship with other Christians
8. You must believe God in His Word
9. You must win souls
10. You must study the Scripture at all times
11. You must be available

In standing for God we are not to look back or sideways or be distracted with other things. There is a saying which goes this way, forward ever in the Lord and backward never in the Lord. In your confession then, you and I should see God as the Almighty God, Everlasting King, the I am that I am. The Prince of Peace, King of Kings, Alpha and Omega, the beginning and the end, our Savior, our Deliverer, and someone Whom you love and you would like to know more about this individual. It is God's desire that we know Him through His only Son, Jesus Christ. Loving God starts with loving His Son, Jesus Christ. Let me ask you another question, Do you love God?

God has called you to surrender your life over to Him. This should be your number one priority in life, not only to give your life to Him, but also to look unto Jesus as the author and finisher of your faith. Do it! Your belief and faith are the tools that should propel you to focus your attention on Jesus Christ. Apostle Paul shed light on this when he said to his audience, "Looking unto Jesus, the author and finisher of our faith who for the sake of joy that was set before Him endured the cross, despising the shame, and set down at the right hand of the throne of God." Hebrews 12:2

Beloved, Jesus Christ is a clear example of how to stand for God. He stood in obedience to fulfill the message for which God sent Him to the earth, which is to save the world from sin. The ultimate result of what Christ did was eternal life in Him. The joy of a true born again Christian is as a result of hope of eternal life which God gave to Christians through Jesus Christ. We have joy, the angels are also rejoicing for us as a result of our stand for God through Jesus Christ.

Whenever you stand for God and do what He said in His word, there is always a reward. Part of the reward is joy. The other is peace. Paul gave a little description of the kind of biblical peace we are to experience. He said, "Peace of God that transcends all understanding." Philippians 4:7

All of our circumstances or pain we are going through, rather we are to focus on doing what God said in His word. Have you had a near similar situation in your life? God is available to restore you no matter what. God's abundance of Grace is always readily available for you.

You are also to allow the power of His spirit to portray His characteristic as a believer through you to the unbelievers.

As you trust and obey, He will use you to declare His awesomeness in the world of sin which is also epitomized by the spirit of anti-Christ. The spirit of antiChrist are those who oppose Christ and His teachings. God wants you and I to believe and trust in His Son, Jesus Christ and to share His love for humanity, among nations, tongues and in all places. Obviously, sharing Christ to others who have not known Him is our sole responsibility. Other people worship other objects other than Christ. There are other categories of people which have not been reached out to with the gospel. The church in general has a duty to reach out to these people, precisely that is why you are called to stand for God so He can use you to save these individuals.

Are you sharing the gospel, are you telling other people about Christ? If you don't, now is the hour and season to showcase Jesus to the world. To start, see my book on practical guides for effective evangelism. Listen. As you share the word of God through evangelism and other forms God releases His power so that His word which you speak comes alive and produces results that lead to one being saved.

Men and women who have served God faithfully whom we read about in the Bible have witnessed the demonstration of God's power in every area of their life and other people's lives, this is as a result of their steadfastness in service of the Lord.

Daniel purposed in his heart and before King Nebuchadnezzar and the people of Babylon that he will not defile himself before Babylonian gods. He stood before his God instead of aligning himself with the delicacies of evil tradition of the Babylonians. Daniel 1:8

Who are you standing for? To whom are you paying allegiance? Are you paying allegiance to the God of heaven whose name is Jehovah, or are you paying allegiance to the tradition of the people, or are you paying allegiance to the other forms of gods?

If you decide to stand for God, He will stand for you. He will never leave you nor forsake you. His love will envelop you. God will also give you His grace of favor for obedience, which means you will obey His commandments whether you like it or not, He will speak to you and reveal His mind to you. He will see you as His ambassador. Yes, He will.

# 10 DISTINCT WAYS TO PLEASE GOD

1.   Receive Jesus Christ in your life as personal Lord and Savior. Romans 10:8–9, John 1:12
2.   Have faith in God. Hebrews 11:6

3.  Obedience to His commandments 1 Samuel 15:22
4.  Study the Bible to know Him better
5.  Fear God Psalm 147:11
6.  Matthew 17:5
7.  Attend fellowship of God's people
8.  Worship Him in season and out of season
9.  Love and care for people (just as Christ did)
10. Participate in kingdom building

The only way to please Him is to be obedient to His commandments. Incidentally, obedience to God is the only sure way to tell God you that you love Him.

## HOW IT ALL STARTED
## SIN CULTURE

The sin of Adam was the stigma through which humanity's relationship with God was adulterated and destroyed. Man's fellowship with God was smeared and was completely out of order as a result of sin. Sin is always emphasized in Christendom so as to alert believers and non-believers of the negative effects of sin in our relationship with God. Sin is a disease, it kills and destroys, sin has no relative or brother, sin is wicked, sin does not spare anyone. Matthew 5:30 says, "And if your right hand causes you to sin, cut it off and cast it from you; for it is more profitable for you that one of your members perish than for your whole members perish, than for your whole member cast into hell."

For sin is the full cause of the world's problems, wars, sickness and diseases, are as a result of sin. First it was through sin that humanity was plunged into eternal condemnation which only through confession of faith in the Lord Jesus Christ will it be erased. Secondly, eradication of sins in our lives is the only way through which you and I will have a meaningful relationship with God.

## WHAT IS SIN?

In the biblical context, sin is a transgression against God's moral laws. The originator and the CEO of sin is the devil. Adam and Eve were the first man and woman to sin against God, then sin from them spread to everyone through the blood. (because they are our grandparents). Every human being was born in sin. That is why Paul, speaking to the Romans, said all have sinned and fall short of the glory of God. Romans 3:23.

God's desire is for His children to live a holy life. He does not want us to live in sin. He wants us to live a life orchestrated by His Spirit. He wants us to practice righteousness. 1 John 3:7.

You can make a choice based on your intuition or friends' suggestions, we are all going through issues we shouldn't have gone through because of the ungodly choices we made. That is why in our generation you will see different lifestyles, some of which are clearly seen in the New Age movement and so many other man designed ways which are contrary to God's clearly laid down principles of living. Sin may be committed in thoughts, words or in actions such as immorality or selfishness, sin brings shamefulness to a person. Being harmful or causing alienation might be considered sinful, more so there are other forms of characterization which you and I consider not sinful but before God, in God's eyes, it is. This is particularly seen in the culture and behavior of people in a community.

The Bible made us understand that God hates sins but loves sinners. Sins are like a large gully between God and man, in analogy you cannot cross the gully to the other side. Sins are impediments that derail us each time you and I want to reach out to God in prayer. Sin distances us from His presence and hinders us from receiving from Him. No wonder God spoke through prophet Isaiah, "Behold the Lord's hand is not shortened, That He cannot save, nor His ears heavy that He cannot hear. But your iniquities have separated you from your God, And your sins have hidden His face from you, So He that He will not hear. For your hands are defiled with blood and your fingers with iniquity; Your lips have spoken lies, your tongue has muttered perversity." Isaiah 59:1–3

These are pretty strong words from God Himself. His intentions have always been to provide, protect and heal us from every kind of sickness and disease. God always wanted to meet our needs. You see, most times we pray and ask God for certain things, and when we don't receive it, then we become upset or we fall into a pity party kind of emotions. We may feel that God did not answer us. But the ultimate truth is that He answers us immediately but the major obstacle is you or I. We are hindered by the sins in our lives. Most times we throw the blame on Satan. Yes, Satan is the reason but we are the ones who gave him the tools to hinder the result of our prayer, we live in SIN OR UNCONFESSED SINS. We are to practice to live holy lives for the Lord, however, if we dabble into sin, confess it immediately according to Romans 1:9 and begin to live for the Lord. Satan has no power to harm you if you lobby God's commandments.

## GOD'S LOVE

God's love for you can never be measured. It is not a friendly love, it is not an infatuation type of love, it is not parents or husband and wife's love, it can never be measured or equated with any kind of affections. "It is known as AGAPE LOVE." Agape love can be described as "UNMERITED KIND OF LOVE," meaning we do not deserve it, there is nothing we can do or something we have done to deserve it, it is a love enveloped within the nature of God Himself. God's love is expressed in the Bible according to the book of John; FOR GOD SO LOVED THE WORLD THAT HE GAVE HIS ONLY BEGOTTEN SON SO THAT WHOEVER BELIEVES IN HIM SHOULD NOT PERISH BUT HAVE EVERLASTING LIFE." John 3:16.

God did not start loving you now, He did not start loving you from your mother's womb, God loved you before the creation of the world. The love of God for you and I had already been established before the world came to be.

Prophet Jeremiah was right when he reminded us this from what God said in His word, "Before I formed you in the womb I knew you. Before you were born I sanctified you; I ordained you a prophet to the nations." Jeremiah 1:5.

## EFFECTS OF SIN

God loves you but hates sin in you. The punishment for sins is death Scripture said. Sin can result in physical death. It can also result in spiritual death. Physical death is the separation of soul from the body, spiritual death is the separation of soul from God. The worst devastating situation in one's life is if your soul is separated from God. Separation from God means admission to the kingdom of Satan. What do you choose, to belong to God or to belong to Satan, the choice is yours.

Apostle Paul said to his audience, "For the wages of sin is death and the gift of God is eternal life in Christ Jesus our Lord." Romans 6:23.

You see, it was God's decision to save humanity from this horrible behavior called "SIN." Yes, He chose to save us. God did what no man can do. If you give yourself some mental exercise of what God thinks about you, I sincerely believe that the Holy Spirit will reveal to you that God loves you unconditionally, and that the cross is where your debt was settled once and for all. THE CROSS of Jesus Christ is one of the evidence of God's love for you and your family. (See the topic on the cross)

But God chose to save us by sending His only begotten son Jesus Christ to come to the earth and die on our behalf, He took our sins on Himself and died on the cross fulfilling the requirement needed for us to be free from the bondage of sin. A righteous person dying for the unrighteous. After three days in the grave He rose again. He is alive today. Paul in his letter to the Romans said, "God demonstrated His love towards us in that while we are yet sinners Christ died for us." Romans 5:8.

## VICTORY THROUGH THE CROSS

As already mentioned, Jesus Christ took all of humanity's sins and nailed them to the cross. He paid the price demanded for us to be free, that is death at the cross. We are free as a result of this. You and I are free today because of the sacrifice Jesus Christ made at the cross. Satan and all that characterizes him lost, but we gain. We have victory over Satan and his allies, you and I are free forever. The moment you come to the realization that you are no more in bondage over sickness, disappointment, failures and other characteristics of Satan, then your life will run in the smooth path intended for you by God.

## JESUS' DIVINITY

Jesus is God.
Jesus is a man.
Before we go into full discussion of the cross of Jesus Christ, let us shed light on the divinity of Jesus Christ as man and as God.

## JESUS CHRIST IS GOD IN THE FLESH

One of the convincing evidences of Jesus as God is found in the miracles He performed. Eight points:

1. He raised the dead from the dead (Lazarus)
2. Gave sight to the blind
3. Fed 5,000 people with two loaves of bread and five fishes
4. Turned water into wine
5. Healed all manner of sicknesses and diseases
6. Delivered those who are bound to some kind of devil
7. He was raised from the dead

Some of these creative miracles made Jesus Christ God in the flesh.
To be seen as God means that He did what no one else could do.
The book of John gave us more dimensional proof of the divinity of Jesus as God and as man. John clearly stated, "In the beginning was the word and the word was with God, and the word was God." John 1:1
Furthermore, He was in the beginning with God. All things came into being through Him, and without Him nothing came be. Moreover, Jesus fed five thousand people with only five loaves of bread. Another amazing miracle was the resurrection of Lazarus from the dead.

## 5 SIGNS OF JESUS CHRIST'S DIVINITY

His divine birth. The paternity of Jesus Christ is one the world sees as a controversial belief, even in some Christian churches which are not spiritually balanced and still disbelieve Jesus' divinity. Other non-Christians do not believe in Jesus' claim of His divinity. The book of Matthew, and Mark, both spoke boldly on Jesus' birth. "The Holy Ghost shall come upon thee and the power of the most high shall overshadow thee."

Jesus Christ cried out in His last hour on earth, it is "FINISHED!" Finished is a significant word in the life of a believer. No more sacrifice of animal blood. Jesus shed His blood once and for all for humanity.

The cross of Jesus Christ is a place of sorrow, a place of sorrow because of the most excruciating pain that led Jesus to cry out, "Father, why has thou forsaken me?" He was abandoned both from God and the world. No one has ever done what Jesus Christ did for the entire world. The cross is also a place of victory, because that is where my sins and yours were permanently defeated. ("O Death, where is your sting? O Hades, where is your victory?) 1 Corinthians 15:55

The ultimate truth, beloved, is when you and I are forgiven from our sins, we are set free. "He who the son of man set free is free indeed," the scripture says. You are living with the hope of eternal life, which is the product of the sacrifice Jesus made for you on the cross.

Jesus Christ is a gift given to mankind. He is the Savior of the world,
He is the way to eternal life,
He is the truth, and He is the life.
He is life given to a dying world.

God gave humanity a special gift in the person of Jesus Christ, and said that those who want life should come to Him. Have you come to Him? Coming to Him is the most important single decision you will ever make in your entire life.

## WHAT'S NEXT?

"Let us hear the conclusion of the whole matter. Fear God and keep His commandment; for this is the whole duty of man." Ecclesiastes 22:13

As already mentioned, inviting Jesus Christ into your life as personal Lord and Savior results in a new relationship with God. Relationship with God is the reason Jesus Christ came to the earth. The scripture says, You are born again. You are a new creature with no sins. The blood of Jesus Christ clears the sin you inherited form Adam. Jesus Christ is like a go-between, between man and God. As a result of His sacrificial death on the cross, man now has access to the Almighty God. We cannot go to God on our own except through Jesus Christ. We must come to God through Jesus Christ. That is why we pray thus; "In Jesus Christ's name I pray. Amen."

## THE ONLY WAY TO FREEDOM

Even when the fact is clearly seen through the eye of faith and the testimonies of those with first-hand information of His death and resurrection, yet the enemy keep doubts in the minds of people, and concluding that the sacrificial death of Jesus was a hoax. Disbelieving Christ's sacrificial death on the cross is one of the worst forms of lies of the enemy, Satan. A lot of people are still bound by doubt that they refuse to make Jesus Christ the Lord of their lives. Jesus said, "I am the way, the truth, and the life, no one cometh unto the father but by me." John 14:6

## JESUS CHRIST AT THE CROSS

Jesus stretched His hands that those who want eternal life should come in. Do you want eternal life? Do you want to identify with Jesus Christ? God is more than willing to save you and give you eternal life. Your spiritual journey starts on what the cross meant to you?

The cross is a place of sorrow. Our sins were nailed with Jesus Christ at the cross. Jesus Christ died at the cross. A place of sorrow because Jesus was abandoned by heaven and by the earth, He suffered extraordinary pain that made Him to start looking for His Father in heaven. "Father, why has thou forsaken me?" All of this is as a result of our sins which He had on Him.

The cross is also a place of joy. Our relationship with God was restored. Jesus Christ became our carrier, He carried us in Him to God the Father. There is no more demarcation between man and God. We have access to

God through Jesus Christ. Apostle Paul put it this way, "For you died and your life is now hidden with Christ in God." Colossians 3:3

Therefore, beloved, for you to ENTER HEAVEN WHERE GOD IS, you must FIRST OF ALL Go through Jesus Christ, YOU MUST MAKE JESUS CHRIST THE LORD OF YOUR LIFE.

## JESUS CHRIST IN THE TOMB

Jesus Christ died on the cross as a result of our sin which was on Him. The Scripture says that He cried out and gave up the ghost.

## RESURRECTION OF JESUS CHRIST

Why am I still alive? This has been the most significant question most people ask at some point in their life. Maybe such a question has flashed across your mind. After you become a Christian by making Jesus Christ your Lord and Savior, God has the ultimate right to call you home to eternal life but He did not, He kept you alive. It is absolutely important to know why you are still here despite the fact that you survived an accident, that sickness did not kill you, that a drive-by shooter did not get you, instead he got someone else. People whom you were born the same year or season have passed but you are still here. When my mom was still alive, when someone died whom she knew she most times came to the conclusion that all her age mates had died and that she was still here. Sometime ago I was talking to my classmate who lives overseas, some of our classmates whom I remembered he would tell me had passed. But we are still here in good health. As already said above, why am I still alive, why are you still alive, why is God still keeping us alive? The obvious reasons can be considered as

1.  Perhaps the most obvious reason is to teach the coming generation about God. God said in the book of Genesis that the reason He kept Abraham alive is to teach his children and his grandchildren the way of the Lord.
2.  God wants us to share the good news of salvation with people who do not know about Him. Mark 16:15, Matthew 18:28:1–

20. Basically, the Bible is filled with God's commandment to go and share the good news who people who have not heard it.

Steps to eternal life:

1.  Believe that you are a sinner.
2.  Confess and repent from your sins
3.  Invite Jesus Christ into your life as personal Lord and Savior.

As already stated, the Bible declares that if you confess with your mouth and believe in your heart that God raised Jesus Christ from the dead, you shall be saved. Romans 10:9

If you made the above statement and invited Jesus into your heart, the Scripture states that you will be saved.

What does this mean to you?

> It means that you belong to God Almighty
> It means that you have been grafted into the family of God
> It means that you are God's child
> It means that you are indwelled by His Spirit
> It means you are elected of God
> It means that the power and anointing of God is on you

## YOUR RESPONSIBILITY

Everyone who has invited Jesus Christ in his or her life as Lord and Savior has a calling to stand for God. You have a duty to perform, you have a well decorated office and all the equipment you need to perfume such duty is available to you through the power of the Holy Spirit.

Your duty post is the area God called you to in the ministry, my duty post is in the street and door to door evangelism. If you call me to be a pastor, I will not function at all. Evangelism is my duty post.

The first step into mastering your duty is your absolute surrender to the Lord Jesus Christ as your personal Lord and Savior. Not only did God assign you as one of His elect, but He also called you His disciple.

Who is a disciple? A disciple is one who follows in his master's footsteps, does everything his master does, is tutored under his master, obeys him at all costs, and obeys all his commandments. Obedience to Jesus' commandments makes you His disciple. Jesus is the master of everyone who confesses Him as their Lord and Savior.

## YOU ARE COMMISSIONED

Many Christians do not know the status of their relationship with God, and as a result of their ignorance they jump from one church to the other or from one ministry to another. Such an ignorant behavior tempts them to build up some negative emotions towards the things of God. The Scripture says that you are called before your conception even took place.

God commissioned you for His services. Yes, you are enlisted into the heavenly armies of Jesus Christ to preach the good news of salvation through which those who hear and believe will have the hope of eternal life in Christ.

The objective of this book is to educate or inform the believers in the Lord Jesus Christ, and non-believers that once you come to Christ by faith, you are spiritually equipped to stand and be one of the apologists of the gospel of Jesus Christ. No matter the situation you find yourself in, or where you are, always remember that you are God's number one choice. you are an elect of God Himself. He called you His child, the scripture says, "As many as receive Him He gave the right to become a child of God, even to those who believe in His name." John 1:12

Listen, God gave you the power to call Him "Abba," which is "Father" and that means you are His child!

## YOU ARE CALLED

A lot of our Christian brothers and sisters do not know that God has placed a calling in their lives. This ignorance has robbed them the joy and other benefits one enjoys knowing the Lord. God issued your calling before the foundation of the world. The book of Jeremiah chapter 1:5 sats, "Before I formed thee in the belly I knew thee, and before thou cometh

REV. DR. CHRIS OKEKE

forth out of the womb I sanctified thee and ordained thee the prophet of the nations."

As already discussed, God called you to be part of His family, you have certain qualities that no other person has. He also entrusted you some responsibilities to accomplish while you live.

When an employer gives you a job, he expects you to do the job for which you are hired, you are not to sit around doing nothing. God wants you to get involved doing the work of God for which He elected you. You are commissioned and equipped to do whatever you are presently doing for Christ.

Whatever assignment you are commissioned to do in the church must be that which points heaven to the hearers. God anointed you for the work He called you to do. Do you feel anointing in your life? God knows you and knows when you are sincere in carrying out your responsibility. God does not play games.

Sometime ago I went on vacation. One of my plans was to do massive evangelism when I got there, I even had some tracts I was going to give out just to continue with the work of God. When I got there I was not able to fulfill my obligations and keep my promise to do evangelism and share some of the tracts. This failure resulted in me being spiritually dry, and it took me a lot of man hours to get up when I came back to my station. If you were to plot a spiritual graph on your service to the Lord, you will find out that it is never straight all through, sometimes it is curved and other times it bends.

In our spiritual dryness we cry out like the Psalmist, "O God, you are my God; Early will I seek you; my flesh longs for you in a dry and thirsty land where there is no water. So I have looked for you in the sanctuary, To see your power and your glory." Psalm 63:2

In my desperation I called upon God and He forgave me for my failure to carry out my assignment, and I have continued to serve Him as He makes His grace available for me.

The point I want to make is that your calling into ministry is a continuous process. If you travel, your assignment goes with you, wherever you are He is there with you to honor His word. Our calling is like an airplane which must continue flying to keep it functional. When it discharges passengers at JFK it is loaded back up to take another journey to other nations. if you let it sit for some time it may need a total overhaul before it flies again.

If you are not active in your calling, then go to God in prayer, and He will refresh you by His Spirit. He did that to me and empowered me again to continue in my area of calling.

Whatever thing you are doing for the Lord, be it pastoring, evangelizing, Bible teaching, gospel singing, Christian counseling, whatever it is, the Scripture says do it as unto the Lord. Secondly, do such responsibilities in a manner that your audience may see the glory of God in it, which may lead them to confess Jesus Christ as Lord and Savior.

Is your work for the Lord leading people to heaven or leading them to hell?

It is absolutely important to evaluate our work with the Lord and ask God questions and ask for His grace to continue in our calling.

We have responsibility from God and to the world. Such responsibilities are also explained by Prophet Ezekiel. "I have made you watchman for the house of Israel, therefore you shall hear a word from my mouth and warn them for me. When I say to the wicked. 'O wicked man, you shall surely die! and you do not speak to warn the wicked from his way, that wicked man dies in his iniquity; but his blood I will require at your hand. Nevertheless, if you warn the wicked to turn from his way and he does not turn from his way, he shall die in his iniquity; but you have delivered your soul." Ezekiel 33:7–9

This is one of the chapters and verses of the Bible in which many preachers failed to warn the congregation of the consequences of not sharing the gospel.

A theological explanation of a watchman is a child of God who was entrusted to take the gospel of Jesus Christ to people and warn them of the consequences of failure to make Jesus their Lord and Savior. This responsibility is for the church. You are a watchman, failure to warn the people attracts God's wrath on us. Get involved in sharing the gospel (evangelism).

## A CHOSEN GENERATION

The Scripture says that, you are a chosen generation, a royal priesthood, a peculiar person. You are not an ordinary person, you are royalty.

You are on a rescue mission for God. You are called and elected before the foundation of the world to stand for the salvation of your soul and other people. God sent you as a light in great darkness, so through you the darkness of sin which engulfs the people will be dispelled.

God is so concerned about you. He came for you, me, and the whole world. He wants us to be holy. He wants us to be perfect children of God. He wants us to be righteous. The Epistle of John declared, "Those who practice righteousness are righteous because he who called them is righteous." 1 John 3:7

You are not an ordinary person, beloved, you are God's child. Lift up your head and dwell in His righteousness!

## DOCTRINE OF ELECTION

Theological definition of election says that God elected or chooses a particular person or group of persons for certain responsibilities. Those elected or chosen are expected to stand for God and for the things of God. "Standing for God" in this context means standing in faith and allowing action to complement your faith in others to achieve result.

Mathematically, it goes like this, FAITH + ACTION = God answers yes and the desired result is achieved.

In context, elect, choose, called, and appointed, all have the same meaning, and serve the same purpose depending on the context for which you want to use any of them. So, therefore, I may mix the words as we proceed in our discussion of the doctrine of election.

In every generation God elects men and women to stand in faith for Him. God must always have someone to stand for Him. That someone is given

1. The responsibility of reaching the world with the gospel message of Jesus Christ
2. To reconcile the world to God
3. To bring the peace and joy of God to the people
4. To take care of God's inheritance (both physically and spiritually)
5. To shine the light of the gospel in the world of darkness

## JESUS CHRIST DECLARED HIS MISSION

Jesus speaking to His audience in one of His crusades said, "The Spirit of the Lord is upon me because He has anointed me to preach the gospel to the poor. He has sent me to heal the broken hearted.

To proclaim liberty to the captives. And recovery of sight to the blind. To set at liberty those who are oppressed. To proclaim the acceptable year of the Lord." Luke 4:18–19

Jesus Himself has a descriptive responsibility of His coming. It all aligned in this Luke 4:18–19. Therefore, beloved of God, whatever Jesus did when He was physically present on the earth is incidentally our calling today that is our responsibility as a minister. Our calling must align with Jesus' ministry. This means that is our calling. Have you discovered this truth about your calling?

Reconciliation is the restoration of friendly or brotherly relationship. God wants to restore humanity to Himself. We were all separated from Him as a result of our sin. It is important to understand that that was the reason Jesus came to the world. He came and was crucified on the cross as a requirement for our freedom from the bondage in which our sins held us. The only way to participate in what Jesus did is to accept the offer by receiving Jesus in our life as Lord and Savior. When we do this, we are cleansed and He owns us. In addition, He delegates some responsibility which we have already discussed above.

We are totally elected to stand for God. Have you ever reasoned in this direction? The scripture calls all the elected children of God "Ambassador." We are ambassadors for Christ. Ambassador will be fully explained separately as we proceed in this discussion.

The first step towards being an elected one is to receive Jesus Christ by faith in your life as your personal Lord and Savior. "If you confess with your mouth the Lord Jesus Christ and believe in your heart that God has raised Him for the dead, you hall be saved." Romans 10:9

This action gives you the hope of eternal life in Him. Not only making yourself available for the service for God but also you become His child. He now sees you are His child. "To them that receive Him He gave them right to become the children of God." John 1:12.

You are now grafted into the family of God as a result of your action. This is very important since it shows our participation in the sacrificial death of Jesus Christ on the cross. Making Jesus Christ your Lord and Savior is the key to obedience to God's commandments.

Then, the second step is to explore who He is in His word, the Bible teaches. The Bible, the word of God, is majorly the avenue through which you can explore who God is and His principles. One of the things we try to emphasize to the new converts us to study the Bible daily. If you are diligent and steadfast in your study of the Bible, then you will have steady spiritual growth. The scripture says, "Study to shew thyself approved unto God, a workman that needeth not to be ashamed, rightly dividing the word of truth." 2Timothy 2:15.

As you faithfully obey Him, He prepares you as one of the elect. God prepares you so you can be able to handle the responsibility He will entrust you to accomplish. Yes, preparation is one of God's choices to get you ready for heavenly assignments.

God's preparation is not easy, it comes through various forms of trials and temptations. James gave us a clear counseling on trials and temptations; "Count it all joy my brothers, when you meet trials of various kinds, for you know testing of your faith produces steadfastness." Verse 4 of the same chapter says, "But let patience have its perfect and complete work, lacking nothing." James 1:2–4

You see, God uses some trials we go through as a testing of our faith, and it is a moment after it is done, that we experience spiritual growth and sharper experience for the things of God. Every experience we get during a testing period is a preparation to stand for God.

Some give their life over to the Lord but most of them cannot stand for Him. Those who can stand for Him have some special qualities, in essence most people received Christ as Lord and Savior but fail to obey Him in all He commanded. The result of disobedience to what He said is the fact that they may not enjoy the benefits that follow obedience as they live their CHRISTIAN life here on earth. If they die they will go to heaven. David was right when He said in the book of Psalms 84, "I'd rather scrub floors in the house of my God than be honored in the palace of sin." Categorically, scrubbing a floor is like a lowly job description, so David was trying to say that he would rather scrub floors than aspire to be in any other higher job description if it means being outside of God's will. So this takes us to the ultimate question.

## EQUALITY BEFORE GOD

God sees everyone equal, both big and small, rich and poor, we are all equal in God's eyes. He loves us equally with His agape love. We differ in the level of faith and sacrifices we render to the Lord in Christ Jesus, so therefore, some have strong faith that can bring results. That is the strongest kind of faith. The scripture says, "So Jesus said 'Because of your unbelief, for assuredly I say to you if you have faith as a mustard seed, you will say to this mountain move from here to there; and it will move, and nothing will be impossible for you.'" Matthew 17:20

God sees us in every aspect of relationship with Him. Before God we are all equal in His eyes. We are, however, all at a different level of service for Him. Everyone will receive reward according to his dedication and sacrifice he has made.

If everyone is equal in our service to Him, it then means that we have no one to look up to for motivation and encouragement, I am not in any way equal in service to those who have given their entire life to the service of God, these ones sacrifice everything they have for God's work. Some have faith in the Lord more than the others, etc. In military circles, there are levels of ranks, they receive these positions according to their merits and qualifications. Some are commanders, majors, colonels, lieutenant generals, some are corporals and so on.

Alternatively, some brethren win more souls than the others, some people have devoted all their lives in service of the Lord. The book of Matthew explains it this way: "For the son of man is going to come with his angels in the glory of his father and then he will repay each person according to what he has done." Matthew 16:27–28.

So, what are you doing as we all live a life of expectancy for the coming of the Lord Jesus Christ?

Jesus Christ revealed to His disciples thus, "Not everyone that saith unto me Lord, Lord shall enter into the kingdom of Heaven, but he that doeth the will of my father who are in heaven." Matthew 7:21

Therefore, we are to consider the following approach: Obedience.

Obedience simply means complying with orders or following instructions stipulated by someone else. It can also mean submissiveness to someone's will. God expects us to follow His orders as written in the Bible. Yes, obedience to what He said is the key to touching the heart of God.

Not everyone can stand for God, but those who make themselves available to Him. One of the main responsibilities God called you for is to send you to the unbelievers to introduce God's love to them through which they will have the gift of eternal life.

God wants to save His people from their sins, God wants to declare to the world His awesome personality through which they come to experience His love in abundance.

In the Bible from Genesis to Revelation, it recorded people that were elected to serve the Lord. Abraham, Moses, Elijah Elisha, Joshua, Nehemiah, Paul, Matthew, John are some of the people we know that God called to stand for Him in all aspects of worship.

The New Testament election is based on your confession of Jesus Christ as Lord and Savior. He called you and I for the same purpose for which He called others, which is to stand for God in obedience to His awesomeness.

These faithful ones stand for God and the things of God. When you stand for God He will lift you up and reveal to you His secrets. The Bible is right when He said that the secrets of the Lord are revealed to His children, you and I and other faithful ones. Relatively, those who have made Jesus Christ their personal Lord and Savior have answered the call of God in their life to stand for Him. They are elected.

The ultimate question is why does God elect these individuals? The same reason He elected them was the same reason He elected you. God elected you and I as an act of His saving Grace (Ephesians 2:8). Grace is defined as unmerited favor.

We do not deserve to be saved as a result of our sins, but He chose to save us because of His Love for us. The cross of Jesus is ultimately the evidence of His love for us.

He wants you stand for Him and for you to be the channel through which He will build His kingdom of God on earth. Jesus Christ hinted at this when taught His disciples how to pray and said, "Thy kingdom come, as is in heaven give us this day our daily bread...."

Everyone elected is meant to stand for God in obedience to His words at all times and continue to share the gospel message to the world.

## YOU ARE ELECTED

I was living a life of sin doing my own things until God in His infinite mercy showed up specifically for me. Not only did He show up in my life, but He chose and elected me to a specific office which by His Grace I am still there.

It is absolutely important for you to see yourself as an elect of God. You do not need someone to remind you or prophesy over you, for you to know that God called and elected you by His Son, Jesus Christ. The book of Jeremiah as already mentioned revealed this truth, then in John 15:16 confirmed the same truth, "You did not choose me, but I choose you and appointed you that that you might go away and might bear fruit and that your fruit might remain, that whatever you may ask in my name the father will give you."

Your election began immediately when you gave your life over to the Lord Jesus Christ. Apostle John declared, "But as many as receive Him, to them He gave the right to become children of God, to those who believe in His name." John 1:12

God elected you to stand for Him in all five aspects as mentioned.

The book of Jeremiah speaks directly to you: "Before I formed you in the womb, I knew you; Before you were born I sanctified you; I ordained you a prophet to the nations." Jeremiah 1:5

The above mentioned book is the scriptural passage that informed you that you are called to the service of the Lord. You can go through it again to let it sink into your memory.

# What God Expects from You

The most important assignment for those who are called by God through Jesus Christ is to stand for Him at any given time in their life's spiritual and physical journey. We may face crises in life, tribulations and other occurrences that may show up, uncertainty and uncomfortable periods may arise. Wars, death, unstable health concerns, poverty, and other unpredictable moments may show up. In the midst of all these circumstances, the questions remain:

What do you do and who do you run to?

Who do you trust to deliver you?

In any and every challenge we may face, God wants you and I to do these five things:

1. BELIEVE HIM
2. TRUST HIM
3. LISTEN TO HIM
4. OBEY HIM
5. HAVE FAITH IN HIM

If you apply these five principle elements in the midst of any challenge you may be going through, God will stand for you according to His promise in Isaiah 43:2, "when you pass through the waters I will be with you, when you pass through the rivers they will not sweep over you. When you walk through the fire you will not be burned, the flames will not set you ablaze."

No circumstances nor any affliction will be able to consume you or overtake you and your loved ones. In practice, it means that you have actually handed over these issues to the Lord.

There is a beautiful song we sang after we prayed over a situation to cease bothering us and seemed immovable. This song expresses the stand of a Christian after we have done all that we can. The lyrics to the song say:

> LIVE IT THERE
> LIVE IT THERE
> TAKE YOUR PROBLEMS
> TO THE LORD
> LIVE IT THERE
> HE WILL SURELY
> DELIVER YOU
> IF YOU PUT YOUR TRUST
> IN HIM
> TAKE YOUR PROBLEMS
> TO THE LORD
> LIVE IT THERE

God is not a man that He will lie nor the son of man that He will repent, Has He said a thing and did not bring it to pass?

Whatever He said in His word concerning you will surely come to pass. If you apply these five principles as stated above, you will see God's promises according to the book of Isaiah which says, "Fear not for I have redeemed you; I have called you by your name, You are mine. When you pass through the waters I will be with you, And through the rivers, they shall not overflow you, when you walk through the fire you shall not be burned or shall the flame scorch you. For I am the Lord your God." Isaiah 43:1c-2d

God is working 24/7 for you. He Will not allow these evil circumstances to consume you or your loved ones, the reason being that you are walking in the revelation of His word, also you are standing for God and walking in obedience to His commandments.

Life is full of trials and tribulations here on this side of eternity. Whatever negativity you are experiencing at the moment, was allowed by God and through it He will bring spiritual increase that will glorify His name. Yes, trials will occur. It is part of the package that constitutes the world. Jesus speaking to His audience said, "These things I have spoken to you that in me you have peace; in the world you have tribulations, but be of good cheer, I have overcome the world." John 16:33

When you focus on Jesus Christ and obey Him in His word, trials and tribulations will occur, yes, some of the trials are to build up your faith. But in all, God will be by your side so the tribulations will not consume you.

It is not easy to live through unpleasant situations or anything that navigates our lives opposite of what God ordained it to be. Anything that negatively affects our naturally ordained livelihood tries to challenge our faith. I believe that's not what you will want. Any issues which affect our lives also affect the level of our faith in the Lord. But if we trust Jesus, He will use the particular situation to catapult our faith in Him to a level of acceptance in Him. He will walk and talk with you even in the midst of the situation. What a beautiful thing to know. Jesus constantly reminds us that we are His own. Jesus is for me. Can you boldly say that Jesus is for you?

It is only faith in Him that will carry you through any circumstances and situations that negatively affect your emotions. If God is for you, who can be against you? No storm, no circumstances or situation will ever succeed in your life, yes, this so true if you choose to stand for Him only.

Some tough times that may affect your emotions include:

- Loss of a loved one
- Loss of a job
- Lack of peace,
- A stormy time in your marriage, or other family issues
- Injury or illness
- Rebellious children

- War
- Poverty.
- Finances
- Troubled child
- Divorce
- Natural causes
- Others

## GOD'S GREAT ASSURANCE IN TOUGH TIMES

In these tough times, the hope and assurance we have is only in the word of God. "HOPE" means a feeling of expectation and desire for certain things to happen. Whenever a Christian is going through tough times, his only hope is in God to bring deliverance. The word of God is the only avenue through which you can survive any tough season. God expects you to claim your victory daily and constantly study the word of God, believing it and walking in it, and claim it as it relates to your circumstances. God is the solution to life's problems, therefore seek Him through the pages of the Bible. We can find what He says concerning a situation and receive the comfort He offers.

1.   God is aware of everything you're going through, He watches over you day and night, His Spirit indwells you to walk with you and comfort you. In fact, prophet Jeremiah says that God knows you before He brought you into this world, if He knows you before you were born, He also knows you after you were born. He watches over you to confirm the truth of His word in you. The Scripture puts it this way, "Before I formed you in the womb I knew you, before you were born I sanctified you; I ordained you a prophet of the nations." Jeremiah 1:5

God also spoke to you and I through prophet Isaiah: "See, I have engraved you on the palms of my hands; your walls are ever before me." Isaiah 49:16

Moreover, Isaiah 41:10 says, "I have chosen you and have not cast you away: Fear not, for I am with you: Be not dismayed, for I am your God. I will strengthen you. Yes, I will I will help for you. I will uphold you with my righteous right hand…"

How glorious it is to know that God knows you and all the things you are going through. He knows when you are sad, and He is aware when your friend is trying to take advantage of you. God knows all about you because He is almighty, omnipotent, omniscience God. He loves you beyond measure, and is always willing to protect you from all kinds of danger, that is why you should determine to hold tight unto Him in faith. He will never turn His back on you. David testified about God, saying, "since I was young but now I am old, I have never seen the lord forsaken the righteous" (emphasis mine). He constantly whispers to your spirit, that He loves you and wants you to trust Him, listen to Him, and obey Him. He wants to finish the work He started with you. He will not let you to go through any form of distress alone. His Grace is always at work in your life and your family.

Obviously, when you stand for God through the above mentioned 4 steps approach, God will immensely respond to you in such amazing ways that releases the fresh anointing that brings breakthroughs in your life.

It is also important to note that you are indwelled by the Holy Spirit whose job is to bring the best of godly living in you and also help you walk in Jesus Christ's footsteps. His divine presence in you is evidenced when you give your life totally for Him and walk in His footsteps. His Spirit whispers in your spirit God's intentions for you and His affirmation of His love. No wonder His word says, "Stand still and know that I am God." Yes, God wants you to listen to Him. He has some specific things to say to you. He needs your undivided attention. Moreso, God wants you to participate in what He is doing in your generation, which is primarily to announce the good news of salvation of your soul to the world. Jesus declares to the people His assignment which is to be completed while He is still in the world. The gospel of Luke puts it this way: "The Spirit of the Lord is upon me, because He has anointed me to proclaim the good news to the poor. He has sent me to proclaim freedom to the prisoners and the recovery of sight for the blind, to set the oppressed free to proclaim the year of the Lord's favor." Luke 4:18–19

The question for you is, do you know your assignment? Can you boldly say Jesus' assignment is your own assignment? For your ministry to be effective it must align with Jesus' ministry. You must love what Jesus loved; Jesus loves people, whom He refers to as inheritance, and Jesus loves His inheritance. You must love people and reach out to them with the love of God which is in Christ Jesus.

As already mentioned above, the salvation of the soul of man is the primary reason Jesus came to the world. To restore our relationship with the Almighty God. To give life to people who are spiritually dead. To give us eternal life. Eternal life without end.

It is absolutely important to know the reason why to deny yourself to follow God.

This is God's testimony. The Scripture says that God so loved the world that He gave His only begotten Son that whosoever believeth in Him should not perish but have everlasting life. John 3:16

We also read, "The thief comes in order to steal, kill and destroy; I have come so that they may have life and that they may have it to the full." John 10:10 (NIV)

As already stated, God knows all about you, He knows all that you are going through. God is much nearer to you than you can ever imagine. If you are going through any uncomfortable situation. which we all do, He is right there to see you through, that is why you will ultimately stand for Him. God wants to heal you, He wants to fight your enemies for you, He wants to give you victories in every circumstance life.

The victory for you is already established through the cross of Jesus Christ, it is an open check, it remains for you to reach out in faith and claim it.

Just write in the open check what you want Him to do for you. The benefits of you standing for Him is one of the obvious reasons He called you His child. He had not called the other persons but you.

In the world of darkness, He called you to be the light, He wants you to shine off the darkness, darkness in the form of sins of disobedience to God's commands, impurity of hearts, idol worships, lies, God gave all of Himself for your sake and mine so that we can stand for Him at any given time in this generation. He also wants you to pass your faith stand action to the next generation, just as we received from those that have passed on. Part of the reason God blessed Abraham was that Abraham will instruct his children and his children's children in the ways of the Lord and teach them obedience. Abraham is the father of all nations.

Also, God wants you to teach your children His ways. Do not hold what you know about God to yourself, pass it on to your children, your children will pass it on to their own children and the process continues until the whole world comes to the knowledge of our lives Lord and savior Jesus Christ.

You are anointed and positioned to engage the totality of yourself in the kingdom building. You are anointed not only to have faith in God but to add action to your faith as well. This process produces a man of God.

We read the Bible written by inspired men and women of God, they encouraged us to demonstrate what we read, i.e. to put what we learnt into action and pass it over to our children and the next generation of God's people.

To stand for God is the number one reason we are alive. Have you ever come to a point in your life where you stand to evaluate your life's spiritual journey. If you do, I believe that the Holy Spirit may have witnessed to your spirit the reason for living. God updates your life daily, giving you and I the opportunity to engage in your calling.

"Through the Lord's mercy we are not consumed, for His compassion fail not, they are new every morning. Great is Thy faithfulness, Oh Lord." Lamentations 3:22–23

The mercy of God refreshes us every morning. Yes, His mercy ushers us into a new life and a new beginning in Him. The first approach of the Christian who understands this revelation is always pray a prayer of thanksgiving and glorifying the name of the Lord as they wake up in the morning. We are to thank God for a new day and a new you. He said, go into this day and be happy in it. We are to start our day with the joy of the Lord in our hearts, because He is with you, walks with you and above all He already took care of our needs for the day. His angels are all around us for services. You and I are victorious children of the Almighty God. God sees us so. Let us see ourselves the way God sees us.

The Scripture declared that we are ambassadors for Christ. Ambassador is one of the most prestigious appointments anyone can get, both here on earth and in heaven. Ambassadors of any nation are treated with dignity and respect, they are like a president of a country. An ambassador represents the president of his country in another country. He relays any information from his country to the country he is residing and from the country he is residing to his own country. He is like a go-between his country and the country where he is residing.

As ambassador, we represent God through Jesus Christ on the earth, we are His hands, legs, everything about Christ. God chose you to be His ambassador. As an ambassador of Jesus Christ, God has given you some specific assignments to carry out. Do you realize that your life is meant to be lived for God alone? God does not want a competition with other entities. God said I am a jealous God. If you truly stand for God, His Spirit will witness to you that you belong to Him. Your Spirit would have agreed with the Spirit of God that you are a child of God.

If you confirm this revelation, then stand for Him in every area of your life, in righteousness, Holiness, Faith, Obedience, literally everything. You are expected to walk in His footsteps. Do you know that you are a unique person with a unique responsibility to serve the Lord? You are the Christ the world is looking at. You are the light chosen to shine off every darkness in the life of God's people.

The Scripture called you the light of the world. The salt of the earth. Your obedience to His word in the Bible is the unique apparatus to prove your love for Him. In addition, see yourself as a new person with a new responsibility of ambassador.

The Scripture says, "Now then, we are ambassadors for Christ; as though God did beseech you by us: we pray you in Christ's stead, be he reconciled to God." 2 Corinthians 5:20

God wants faithful ones who will declare His glory and awesomeness to this generation of His people. When you stand for God, He will use you to draw all men to Himself. God is looking for those people who will trust Him even in the midst of hardships and other difficult circumstances. He is looking for the ones who will occupy the spiritual mansion in heaven. The mansion is not for everyone but for those who will trust Him. Apostle John went ahead to declare what God said: "In my father's house are many mansions; if it were not so, I would have told you. I am going to prepare a place for you. And if I go and prepare a place for you, I will come again, and receive you unto myself; that where I am, there ye May be also." John 14:2–3

God wants to use you to turn the sinners back to His saving Grace. He wants you to make yourself available so you can be a vessel through which He can change the world. God needs you! We are in an urgent period in the history of the world time in which the trumpet may sound that signifies the arrival of our Savior, Jesus Christ. You see, a lot of people, even our Christian brothers and sisters have not come to the realization that we are living in the last days of our lives.

The ultimate questions we ought to ask ourselves is, what I am going to be doing as we wait for the second coming of Jesus Christ?

Matthew 24 declares Jesus' instructions to His disciples; This gospel of the kingdom must be preached preceding His coming back to the earth. In essence, we are to be consistent in sharing the good news of the gospel of the kingdom of God. Sharing the gospel is a universal call to the church. God commanded every Christian to "GO." Go means go, move forward, get out of your comfort zone and go, keep going until He calls you to eternity or He gives you another assignment. Before Jesus gave this commandment, He already provided everything you need to enable you to succeed in the assignment including being your mouthpiece, all you need to do is show up in His presence. Wherever you are teaching, preaching, evangelizing, counseling, etc., His presence, the Holy Spirit is right there with you to confirm His words by signs and wonders. On every occasion when I have the privilege to talk to someone about Jesus Christ, seconds after the ministrations I can't remember the specifics I spoke to the individual. Even if the words are written down, most of the words you spoke are not part of your own notes. What really took place was that the Holy Spirit took over the ministration and spoke the eternal word that convicted the individual.

God does not want anyone to be taken unawares, He wants those who have not repented to repent from their sins; you and I are sent to take His message of salvation to the world. God designed you for this purpose. The question is, are you available for His service? You have to understand that God left heaven and came down for you and I to rescue us from sin and ordained and sent us to rescue others who are about to be thrown into hell fire. God is more serious than we can ever imagine when it comes to bringing the gospel to the population of unbelievers. BE INVOLVED!

This book, "Standing for God," will speak directly to your heart on what it takes to STAND for God. Every paragraph is intended to remind you to stand for God only and be available for His service. Let the Holy Spirit lead you as you read through the pages of this book, "Standing for

God," in the name of Jesus Christ, in a world filled with different elements of opposition to the principles of God laid down for us.

Your action goes beyond your existence here on earth but gives you reward reserved for you in heaven according to 1st Peter chapter one, God sees you as one of His true ambassadors reserved for the season. My question remains: Is God seeing you as His true ambassador? Has the Holy Spirit revealed to you what your responsibility is all about as His true representative.

We cannot navigate other ways to God for God but His ways. Standing for God alone in every area of life is one of the most powerful demonstrations of love and obedience to Him. Yes, when we follow God, He sees us as true believers, He reveals His mind to us and what He wants us to do step by step.

## FAITH IN ACTION

Faith is a major motivating factor if you are willing stand for God.

The Scripture declared in James 2:17, that faith without action is dead. "Faith" and "action" are coined together. Faith in the Lord cannot make you a totally committed Christian, so also "action" alone cannot guarantee you eternal life in heaven.

When you add action to your faith in God it produces results that please the Lord. If someone asks you if you love God you probably say yes, Jesus made a statement concerning the claim that you love Him.

"If you love me, keep my commandments-and I will pray the father and He shall give you another comforter, that may abide with you forever Even the Holy Spirit." John 14:15

God's commandment comprises both faith and action.

1.   PHYSICAL FAITH STANDING (ACTIONS)
2.   SPIRITUAL FAITH ACTION (SPIRITUAL)

## PHYSICAL FAITH STANDING

Physical faith standing action is produced from spiritual faith actions. This category represents the practical ways in which you are engaged in serving the Lord faithfully. Such practical ways include going to places to share the gospel of love of Jesus Christ, handing over tracts to someone to be saved after reading the tracts. Preaching, laying of hands on a person, leaving your comfort zones to another area to counsel a discouraged person, preaching of the gospel both in and out of the church premises, attending to the needy person, etc.

Your spirit which cannot be seen propels the practical faith action to do the work of God in action. If you say that you have faith, then where is the action, man of God? You had faith that God will definitely save or deliver unsaved individuals, you then backed your faith by going to do the action which will actually bring results.

All the men and women of God who has served the Lord faithfully carried out the Lord's commands by backing up their faith by action, that is by doing what was commanded. Your physical actions complement your faith in the Lord's service. These men and women of God were seen as God's generals because their faith which is spiritual was backed up by actions resulting in the immediate move of the demonstration of the power of God.

FAITH IN THE LORD JESUS CHRIST + WORKS (ACTIONS) = MIRACLE

FAITH IN THE LORD MINUS WORKS = ZERO RESULT

"FOR AS THE BODY WITHOUT THE SPIRIT IS DEAD, SO FAITH WITHOUT WORKS IS DEAD." James 2:26

The word of God is God, and God is His word. John 1:12 says, "In the beginning was the word and the word was with God."

God does not differentiate from His word. Nobody has seen God before, so the only way to access Him is through faith in His Son Jesus, and of course your faith is developed from His word.

"Faith comes by hearing, hearing by his word." Romans 10:17

As a child of God, you hear God speaking to you at all times, but the key is to receive what He says and apply it to what it means. The characteristics of those that are serious with God who are ready to stand for Him in faith:

1. They heard the word of God
2. They believed what He says to them

3. They applied faith in what God said
4. They applied action to what God said.
5. God honored His word and the result was achieved

The same result will occur if you stand for God in these five sequences. God is ready to use you beyond measure. He is waiting for your response in the area of availability. Make yourself available by standing for Him in your faith and obedience.

A lot of people would like to stand for God and His purposes but do not know how. Standing for God in faith and applying your faith in your work is not automatic, you cannot achieve it based on your title or education, it is not achieved by attending a large congregation or Bible believing congregation but can be achieved first, by making sure that your relationship with Jesus is that which is born in love.

This issue of loving God must be established by you alone. God loves you unconditionally, period. Do you love Him? Your love for God is seen in your willingness to obey His commandments. Yes, friend, prove your love for God by doing what He asked you to do. Your recognizable love for Him is determined by your obedience to His commandments. Because God loves you, He wants you to grow in your knowledge of Him.

Secondly you must be in the word by studying the word diligently. By this your faith will grow as well without limitations.

Apostle Paul wrote to the young evangelist, Timothy, "Study to show thyself approved unto God, a workman that needeth not to be ashamed, rightly dividing the word of truth. 2 Timothy 2:15

Your relationship with Jesus Christ is something above knowledge, it is a relationship. You may have knowledge but not relation, but if you have relation you can have knowledge as well, relationship is an act of love in its fullness, but knowledge may be only mental accented. So therefore strive to have relationship with Jesus Christ so that you worship will be meaningful.

Thirdly, apply what you learned from your study in your daily living. Always practice doing what the word says. A common saying goes this way, "practice makes perfect." If you practice keeping the word and fail to some extent, do not back out but try again depending on the Holy Spirit who indwells you daily to help you overcome it. He will enable you to grasp it in a heavenly fashion.

Remember, God searches every heart and rewards accordingly, He knows your thoughts, and He knows your love for Him. He also knows if you are willing to have a relationship with Him. He knows the state of mind!

God said to Moses: "I have surely seen the affliction of my people which are in Egypt, and I have heard their cry by reason of their taskmasters; for I know their sorrows, And I am come down to deliver them out of the hand of the Egyptians, and bring them up out of that land unto a good land and a large, unto a land flowing with milk and honey; unto a place of Canaanites and the Hittites and Amorites, and the Perizzites and the Hivites, and the Jebusites. Now therefore behold the cry of the children of Israel is come unto me and I have also seen the oppression wherewith the Egyptians oppress them." Exodus 3:7–8

When Moses heard the word of God instructing him on what to do, he followed the sequence as specified above. Moses heard the word, believed the word, applied his faith and finally he applied action and God honored His word and the children of Israel were delivered from the hand of Pharaoh and his taskmasters.

Moses he believed Him and had faith that God will surely deliver His people from the bondage in Egypt. Then he made himself available for action. First he went to Pharaoh to give him God's instruction. The total emancipation of the children of Israel from Egypt was achieved as a result of Moses' faith in God and his availability to demonstrate God's words to Pharaoh.

As already discussed, you and I are a chosen vessel for the Lord's use. Our life here on this side of eternity is to take care of God's inheritance through which we lift His name high so that others will come to know the true living God.

## STANDING IN FAITH

When you consider spiritually standing for the Lord you think of your faith walk in Him, or spiritual demonstration of your faith. Faith is very important when it comes to serving the Lord. Faith is what makes a person a child of God. Faith in God is what makes our worship worthwhile. It draws us directly into the presence of God.

Without faith in the Lord you cannot represent God in any category of life. All the men of faith in the Bible are people God trusted to obey His commandments. The Scripture validates faith as a means to know God,

The book of Hebrews shed light on it, "But without faith it is impossible to please God, for he that cometh to God must believe that He is a rewarder of them that diligently seek Him." Hebrews 11:6

Faith is not only spiritual but physical. Spiritual faith cannot be touched but it can be demonstrated. To spiritually stand in faith for God means standing and carrying out all His commandments without an iota of doubt. In a situation when others are scared and faithless, you bring words of assurance and trust that what God said, He will bring to pass. When you stand in faith for God, He will in turn bring to pass that for which you are trusting Him. All the prophets in the Bible stood in faith for God, and God through them accomplished great things. Prophets like Moses in the book of an Exodus through whom God delivered the children of Israel from their bondage in Egypt. Abraham is known as the father of faith who believed God for a child, at the old age when all hope was lost he had Isaac with his 90 year old wife Sarah.

## SIN SEPARATES US FROM GOD

The passages of the Bible from Genesis to Revelation echo God's ultimate intentions to bring man back to Himself. Humanity's separation from God started when Adam and Eve disobeyed God's commandment by eating the particular fruit God said do not eat.

This disobedience brought about the separation of man from the presence of God and the fellowship they had on a daily basis. Sin is the only weapon which Satan uses to separate us from the Almighty God. God hates sin and does not have any space for sin to dwell in Him. He is too Holy to behold any kind of sin.

Contrarily, God loves the sinners but does not like the sin in them. Sins carry a heavy weight of consequences, which are both spiritual and physical. Apostle Paul spoke to his audience in Rome thus, "For the wages of sin is death but the gift of God is eternal life through Jesus Christ our Lord." Romans 6:23

## REMEDY FOR SIN

We are supposed to die for our sins but Jesus died on our behalf. The abundance of His love and mercy for humanity took Him to die for us, and He was resurrected on the third day. The righteous died for the unrighteous. Jesus' death on the cross is the ultimate reason for living. We have eternal life because of His sacrifice on the cross.

As already mentioned, God loves us so much and doesn't want us to die and go to hell. His love for us is unconditional, it is agape kind of love. The elites and philosophers who have lived and died including the ones living at the moment could not understand why one person can give his life over the generations of people.

No one who has lived or is still living will be able to explain the love of God for us. 1 John declares, "What manner of love the father had for us that we should be called the children of God and the world did not know us because they did not know Him." 1 John 3:1

## JESUS CHRIST GOT RID OF OUR SINS

We are all sinners by nature. For us to stand for God means that our sins are to be dispensed of. Jesus left heaven for this purpose to deliver humanity, you and I from our sins. Paul speaking to his audience said, "But God proves His love for us: while we were still sinners, Christ dies for us." Romans 5:8

No one in heaven, or on earth or under the earth or anywhere could deliver man from the penalty of sin, but Jesus Christ. It is because of His intervention that we were set free from sin and its consequences. How will you feel to know that you are finally free from all the calamity of sin? Jesus Christ further gave us assurances that even if we sin, He is faithful and just to forgive us our sins and to cleanse us from all unrighteousness (1 John 1:9).

It is your responsibility and my duty to abstain and avoid sin and its likeness. Yes, it is your responsibility to flee from all kinds of sins and its likeness, for sin kills both spiritually and physically.

You know that drinking and smoking is not good for you as a man of God, so why do you hang out with people who smoke and drink?

You know also that day or night clubs have no place in the kingdom of God, why do you hang out there?

Prostitution is evil against your body and also a sin against God, why do you hang out with prostitutes?

The only condition through which you can mingle with sinners is to introduce Jesus to them. Life in Jesus is a new life which they have not experienced before. This is the reason we are called to bring them to the saving grace of Jesus so that they can experience a glorious life which is found in Jesus Christ. Paul said that he can be all things for the sake of the gospel.

I have personally been with drug addicted people and alcoholics just to tell them about Jesus Christ and His salvation message. To witness to this population, you must have a clear-cut objective which is to be given the opportunity to have eternal life. More importantly, you must seek the face of God before witnessing to them.

God can forgive any sin, the word God says that blood cleanses every sin, but the blood of Jesus does not cleanse repeated sins if you persist in them and do not repent. Yes, many times we sin willingly. Sin committed in ignorance is forgiven. Ignorant means lacking in knowledge or information. Yes, if you don't know that the action you did is against God's commandment and went ahead to do it, God forgives, the blood of Jesus Christ cleanses us.

Have you asked for the forgiveness of your sins today? It is absolutely important for you as a lover of God to evaluate your life daily and confess any sin that the Holy Spirit might bring to your attention. Yes, I do evaluate my day before I retire for the night and confess any misdeeds that I might have done during my daily orientations. We are to do personal spiritual evaluation to make sure that we do not harbor sin in our lives. You are to be consistent in this aspect.

Sometime ago I took a pen that does not belong to me from my office. I love to collect pens, especially if it is beautiful. I took the pen, I know very well that it does not belong to me. When I got to my car, on trying to open up my door I heard in my spirit what I believe to be the inner witness of the Holy Spirit saying, the pen you took does not belong to you, I tried to argue but the same conviction kept coming to my mind,. I did not have my peace until I returned the pen to where I picked it up from. I returned the pen as I promised. After I returned it, I felt peace in my Spirit. Now you might say that's an ordinary pen, yes, beloved but God looks into every minute detail in our lives, no matter how significant it might be. God does not want us to be polluted with sins. Paul speaking to his audience in Ephesus said, "That it might present it to himself a glorious church, not having spot or wrinkles, or any such thing, but that it should be holy and without blemish." Ephesians 5:27

The Scripture said that there should be no spots or wrinkles in your garment if you want to make it to the end. Prophet Isaiah further explained it clearer: "Behold the hand of God is not shortened that it cannot save; neither his ear heavy, that it cannot hear, But your iniquities have separated between you and your God, and your sins have hid his face from you, that he will not hear." Isaiah 59:1–2

In simple terms, the word of God said my iniquity, your iniquity and the rest of the world has been the main obstacle to getting our prayers answered. The disobedience of Adam brought calamity to all generations after Adam.

Adam disobeyed God in the garden of Eden by eating the particular fruit that God had commanded him and his wife Eve not to eat (Genesis chapter 3.) The Scripture also informed us that Satan got the man to sin through his wife Eve.

Eve succumbed to the deception of the devil, she then got her husband convinced that the fruit was good to eat, the husband Adam willingly ate the fruit and did not consider God's instruction not to eat the fruit. Obviously, we talk of Adam's disobedience but we have done the same thing over and over again. We know what the word of God said in the Bible but we go and do the opposite, sinning against Him. Sometimes our request from God does not evidence or it is delayed as a result of unconfessed sins. Do you know that your sins can work against you continuously, especially unconfessed sins? Yes, it is dangerous to walk around with sin plastered in your life. Under this condition you will never receive any good thing from the Lord.

Isaiah warns us, "Behold, the Lord's hand is not shortened, that it cannot save, neither his ear heavy, that He cannot hear; But your iniquities have separated you between you and your God and your sins have hid his face from you, that he will not hear you." Isaiah 59:1–2

We will try to draw some points from this Adam and Eve romance with their enemy, the devil.

1.  Adam was not spiritually alert when the devil tempted them. God warned the church through the book of Apostle Peter: "Be sober, be vigilant because your adversary the devil walks about like a roaring lion, seeking whom he may devour." 1 Peter 5:8

Being alert means being in the word of God and meditating on it day and night. Jesus was alert when He was tempted by the devil. Jesus used the word of God to defeat the devil. Without the word of God in our lives Satan will continue to toil with us anyhow. Yes, as a believer the only weapon at our disposal is the word, Jesus Christ, for at His name every knee bows and every tongue confess that Jesus Christ is Lord to the glory of God.

Churches who does not instruct the attendance in the word of God and live in it may not experience the benefits of being in Christ.

2.  We are to apply the word of God in any given situation and circumstances that are working against the purpose of God in our lives and other stressful situations we go through on a daily basis.
3.  As we stand in the victory through the cross, we are to have unadulterated trust in Jesus Christ who gave us the victory.
4.  We are to stand firm in our faith in Him, do not allow any room for compromise.

## SPIRITUAL HEAD OF THE FAMILY

Man is the spiritual head of the family. Unfortunately, a lot of people misunderstood this responsibility. To them, a spiritual leader is one of the elements in the compound family of control, therefore he issues a command to his family or to people he provides for, and expects them to follow his commands.

No one should have the audacity to control any person. A spiritual leader is one who has a relationship with Jesus Christ and follows His ways. Yes, this is so true. One of the characteristics of a spiritual leader is love not only those he leads but others. The Bible teaches that God is love and God is love. Such love He gave to mankind, therefore if you receive Christ as Lord and Savior you receive love, and so you give out love to those you lead. His love is evidence in your lives and will affect everything you do including being a spiritual leader of your family. A spiritual leader leads by the direction of the Holy Spirit of God, and not what worldly counselors or your friends say or do, or how you see others lead. (Control is associated with witchcraft, so avoid it, don't practice it.)

A spiritual leader is spiritually equipped to stand for on behalf of his family and other dependents. These include your community, state, country or nation.

God always has something to say to His people and so He needed someone to take the message to the people, that someone may be you, if you have surrendered your life to Him. All the prophets in the Bible are all leaders and are vessels through which God sends His message to His people. Consequently, it is the spiritual leader's responsibility to see that God's instruction is followed by everyone that is in his care.

What is your position in your family, are you listening to God or are you just existing?

It is your responsibility to pray for your family, that is why it is absolutely important to stand for God and His purposes. Adam was not spiritually alert when the enemy showed up with lies from the pit of hell. We can overcome Satan's deceit by knowing what the word of God says.

We are to stand for God in our faith in Him and receive instructions on how we can prayerfully defend our family and God's inheritance against Satan's attacks. God knows our weakness and our strengths. When Satan comes to attack our families, he first targets the man, the spiritual leader, then he penetrates and causes havoc.

In this context of a spiritual leadership, man represents both genders. Man is absolutely equipped to pray not only for himself but also for his wife and other members of his family.

# CHAPTER 6

# Number One Enemy of Our Faith: Satan

Right from the time Lucifer, (Satan, devil, evil or every other names you may refer to Lucifer) was kicked out of heaven, with the subsequent defeat he suffered at the cross, has not ceased to take his anger and frustration to the children of God. His agenda has not changed or altered, it has always been to

1. To stop man from believing and obeying God's commandments
2. To stop our worship
3. To stop your faith in the Lord

## THE SCRIPTURE DECLARES HIM AS A LIAR AND THE FATHER OF LIARS

John 8:44 says, "Ye are of your father the devil and the lusts of your father ye will do. He was a murderer from the beginning and abode not in the truth because there is no truth in him, when he speaks a lie, he speaks of his own for he is a liar and the father of it."

The major area of his operation is through our mind, he operates in our mind day and night with the main intention to cause us to sin against God. The only proven tool to keep him away from our lives is the word of God. The scriptures said that, Satan came to kill, steal and to destroy. Jesus Christ said, "I am come that they may have life and that they may have it more abundantly." (emphasis is mine) John 10:10

James 4:7 said to us, listen, "Submit yourself therefore to God, Resist the devil, and he will flee from you."

Satan continued to operate through various means including using the wicked side of our lives. As we go on this discussion, we are going to discuss these various enemies in detail.

Satan has continued to present himself as the compound enemy of our faith in Christ. From the time he lied and deceived Adam and Eve to sin against God, he has never ceased to tempt all of humanity, who are the descendants of Adam and Eve, and of course that includes you and I. The troubles which we experience in our lives daily evolved from the sin of Adam and Eve.

I want you to understand that Satan is not happy with you. He hates you, especially when you are called a child of God. A child of God is one who has confessed Jesus Christ by faith as his personal Lord and Savior. The devil attacks the most important part of your connection to God which is your faith. You approach God by faith.

Apostle Paul speaking to the Hebrews, said, "But without faith it is impossible to please Him for he who comes to God must believe that He is, and that He is a rewarder of those who diligently seek him." Hebrews 11:6

We need to have faith in God in other to avoid the onslaught weapons of the enemy.

## LACK OF KNOWLEDGE

Lack of knowledge of the knowledge of God means ignorant, unlettered, uneducated, of what the Word of God said. When you are not detailed in who God is, the enemy takes advantage of your ignorance to rob you from receiving the blessings of God for your life. Moreso you will not enjoy your CHRISTIAN life to the full and may not know what God has in stock for you, including the ultimate blessing of eternal life.

You will be in competition with the world.

You will not be able to share your faith or be an effective apologist for the kingdom of God if any of the above points are not taken. You will be vulnerable in a situation where you are supposed to speak out for Jesus. Lack of the knowledge of God lined up as one the most powerful weapons of Satan to hinder your faith in in Him.

Hosea 4:6 says, "My people are destroyed for lack of knowledge; I will also reject thee, that thou shalt be no priest to me; seeing thou has forgotten the law of thy God, I will also forget thy children."

Apostle Paul speaking to his audience said, "Jesus Christ is the Image of invisible God." Colossians 1:15

Jesus said to His disciples, "Anyone who has seen me has seen the father." (John 14:9b). This was the reply Jesus gave to Philip who asked to see God. Jesus' express answer to Philip gave us insight into who He is. The Scripture informed us that Jesus is God. (John 1:12).

Standing for God means to obey all of His commandments, no matter what come in between you and God. In trial, and in your afflictions. You choose to trust Him.

## SELF

In most cases you are your own enemy. Being your own enemy means that you make decisions which are detrimental to your happiness and what God ordained for your life. The opposite of happiness is sadness. Depending on yourself is trusting your flesh. Flesh demands anything contrary to God's will for your life. Self-will without God is dangerous to your faith in Christ. Any decision without God makes you vulnerable to Satan.

Jesus wants you to be happy at all times. He commanded His children to be happy,

> "This is the day the Lord has made, we will REJOICE AND BE GLAD IN IT." Psalm 118:24
> (See my book on the Joy of Salvation)

## UNAVAILABILITY

I've heard a lot of people say that we are in the computer or microwave age. Our lives run so fast that we don't spend enough time in the word of God. We rush in to pray and rush out to face another lined up program for the day. God is standing to bless is but finds no one on duty. God expects us daily to live for Him. He positioned us to be a praise for Him. We praise the Lord in the way we live our lives, our daily orientations must be that which is orchestrated by the love of Christ, there must be evidence of Christ in us.

A Christian friend testified sometime ago that he spent a lot of time playing gospel music, not much time on the word of God. So he said that God spoke to him that whenever He wants to reveal some important things to him, he is always not available. You see, listening to Christian music is not a bad thing, but sometimes God needs your undivided attention. He needs you to listen to the inner witness of His Spirit for some specific instructions. God needs your attention every day. When God gives instruction He wants it to be carried out before He can give you another one.

## KNOWLEDGE OF GOD

Having a relationship with God through Jesus Christ is the ultimate in practical obedience to God. Knowledge of God is the next important part of doctrine one should embrace. Worship Him. Ultimately, knowledge of Him comes as we engage in His services comes through:

- Studying the word of God, the Bible, and putting what I learnt into practice
- Total obedience to His commandments
- Attend the congregation of other believers where the word of God is heard and taught by a Holy Spirit led teacher
- Attend conventions, seminars, and volunteer to participate in Christian gatherings
- Practice the presence of God in your day to day activities
- Talk to Him and be honest in His presence

- Believe Him in His word
- Share your faith to people who have not heard the gospel
- Give to the poor and the underprivileged in our society
- Be faithful

The Lord looks at the heart of service, He wants to trust and depend on you to reach the rest of the people to save them. As you serve the Lord faithfully so will He reveal His awesome personality to you. He reveals His mind to you and what He intends to do. The faith of Abraham in Him drew His attention to Himself, then He revealed to Abraham that He will make Abraham the father of nations, and that his wife Sarah will bear children to him. Moreover, He will give Abraham a son that will inherit Abraham's wealth.

Knowledge of God does not always come that easy. God will take you through some rounds of tests. God's testing comes with His grace. His grace helps us to stand and do our assignment in the midst of our storms. God said to Paul, "My grace is sufficient for thee for my strength is made perfect in weakness. I rather glory in my infirmities that in the power of Christ may rest upon me." 2 Corinthians 12:9

Increased knowledge of God in Christ Jesus is the ultimate sign of spiritual growth in God because the Holy Spirit takes residence and becomes the government of your life. God desired that we keep growing spiritually in His knowledge. When we have a relationship with God through Jesus Christ then the knowledge of Him follows, as already discussed, the Holy Spirit takes control.

To maintain and nourish our relationship with Jesus we must spend quality time in His word. Many Christians substitute studying and fellowship in the presence of the Holy Spirit with only listening to gospel music, or listening to a favorite preacher. In addition, you are to develop the attitude of studying the word of God and applying what it says in your daily orientations.

God wants to spend quality time with you because He loves you. He wants to speak to you. He wants to be your Father and your God. Invariably, God wants to speak to us in the quietness of our hearts, that is why we have quiet time with Him. He wants to witness in our heart. He wants you to be on your duty post and available for His purpose. We have to be available to go to evangelism, or prayer meetings or visiting the sick, and other similar services for God. Sometimes we find reasons not to be available for God's assignments. Such reasons are part of Satan's strategy to stop us or distract us from obeying God. Our reasons sometimes seemed genuine, but not enough to be unavailable when He needs us for a particular assignment.

## HINDANCES TO KNOWLEDGE OF GOD

### 1. SIN

In general, sin stands out as the most common agent which grossly affects our faith in the Lord Jesus Christ. **SIN IS DISOBEDIENCE TO GOD'S COMMANDMENTS.**

**Every evil that has been affecting Man's well-being is the result of the sin of Adam and Eve. Wars, quarrels, failures, backwardness, anger, are also the result of our sinful nature.**

Sin is a barrier between us and God. God will not hear our prayers as a result of our sin. The book of Isaiah said, "Behold, the hand of God is not shortened, that He cannot save, neither His ear heavy, that He cannot hear; But your iniquities have separated between you and your God; and your sins have hid his face from You, that He will not hear." Isaiah 59 1:2

It is only sin that separates us from the love of God which are in Christ Jesus. The Scripture tells us that we have all sinned and fall short of the glory of God. But there is hope in Jesus Christ. It was our sins that drove Him to the cross, He literally died on the cross with our sins on Him.

Our victory results from Jesus Christ's shed blood on the cross. As a result, we all have access to the throne of Grace of God. Yes, we are no more bounded by sin of Adam. Our acceptance of Jesus Christ as our Lord and Savior and our assurance of what He did at the cross is in place to boost and catapult our spiritual life to a greater level of unshakable faith in the Lord.

We all who know Jesus as Lord and Savior are victorious over the things of the world. The Bible said that we have an advocate who pleads for us if we sin. His name is Jesus Christ, the Son of the living God. In the mercy and love of God for man, God made a way of escape; the book of John puts it this way: "If we confess our sins, He is faithful and just to forgive us our sins and to cleanse us from all unrighteousness." 1 John 1:9

## 2.    FEAR

Fear is an emotional reaction to a feeling that something dangerous is about to happen. Fear is not physical but spiritual. It can also be defined as an unpleasant situation characterized by the perception of danger, real or imagined.

However way we define fear, it is still not a good thing. Fear is a weapon of the enemy which he uses against the believers in the Lord Jesus Christ, to distract them from their faith. Satan has been using this weapon since sin was introduced into the world through Adam and his wife Eve. Satan has used this weapon to destroy a lot of faithful followers of Jesus and reduced them to ordinary faith. Fear creates terror and consequently doubt in your faith walk with the Lord.

Satan's objectives are to paralyze you to the level that you don't even trust yourself. He uses fear to target your faith, he knows that your faith is the key to serving the Lord effectively. There are so many passages of the Bible that command us not to fear The Scripture declares, "But without faith it is impossible to please Him; for he that cometh to God must believe that he is, and that he is a rewarder of them that diligently seek Him." Hebrews 11:6

As already discussed, faith is the key that unlocks all you want to know about God; obviously, then, lack of faith hinders the knowledge of God in the life of a believer.

## HOW TO GET RID OF FEAR

The word of God is the only known key to destroying fear in our lives. First of all, we must remember what happened at the cross in which Jesus Christ delivered humanity from all the negativities that affect our lives including fear. Jesus' final words while He was still on the cross were IT IS FINISHED! That victory belongs to every believer who has faith in Him. We already have victory over fear, death, etc. It covers us in every aspect of our encounter with the enemy including fear. The Scripture said,

"For God has not given us the spirit of fear but of power, and of love, and of sound mind." 2 Timothy 1:7

You are to challenge this spirit called fear with what God said about it.

When you allow fear to torment you even as a believer, you are abjectly proving that you do not have faith in God. Till today, fear is a very powerful weapon Satan uses against the believers in the Lord Jesus.

## ONE WHO CAN STAND FOR GOD

There are certain categories of people who can stand for God. Not everyone who claims to belong to God can stand for Him. These ones have certain qualities.

1.    A personal relationship with Jesus Christ.

Relationship with His Son, Jesus Christ is the first quality God is looking for in a person that will stand for God. The scripture said that, "If you confess with your mouth Jesus Christ and believe in your heart that God raised Him from the dead you shall be saved." (Romans 10:9). The book of John confirms the above statement. "To them that received him, He gave the right to become the children of God."

It then means that as you read or study the word of God, you are actually having a conversation with God. I encourage you to be more dedicated to studying the word of God. There is healing, deliverance, protection, provision, and comfort in the word of God.

Above all, you will begin to look like Him in your conduct. In the New Testament, the people saw how the disciples conducted themselves. I believe they reasoned within themselves and concluded that the disciples look at their master Jesus Christ. And so they said they are Christ like. Obviously, it is important that the church cherish and honor the CHRISTIAN because it was derived from our Savior, CHRIST. As already mentioned, having Jesus Christ in your life as Lord and Savior is the most important decision you will ever make in your life. The Bible declares, "That if you confess with Your mouth the Lord Jesus Christ and believe in your heart that God raised Him from the dead, you will be saved." Romans 10:9

2. Obedience to what God said.

Obedience to God's commandments to His people is one the strongest clues to getting His attention. It is a perfect way to prove your Lord for God. Jesus spoke to His disciples in one of His teachings, saying, "If you love me keep my commandments."

To keep God's commandments you must know what the word said in the Bible, if you do not understand what the word said then it will be hard for you to keep the commandments, then you will also practice to apply it in your life. Every obedience needs practice, if you fail at the initial time, go back and practice again. Remember, God is watching you and knows your heart. He watches you to know how serious you are when it comes to obeying Him.

God wants to make you a great man/woman of God. He wants to use you to do great things for His people.

Moses kept God's commandments, and as a result of his obedience to God's words, God lifted him to a greater spiritual level. He delivered the Israelites from their bondage in Egypt under king Pharaoh. He was honored by the people of Egypt and Israel.

David depended on God and obeyed God's commandments, he revered, he honored the name of the Lord before the Philistine Army and the Israelites. In the battle between them, as a result God made him the king of Israel, God also gave him victories in all the wars Israel fought.

Abraham obeyed God's commandments, God lifted him up and called him God's friend and also father of nations. There are so many other men/ women in the Bible that God lifted their status as a result of their obedience to God's commandments.

The Bible reveals that God is not a respecter of persons, if you obey God's commandments, He will give you spiritual upliftment to stand for Him in this world filled with darkness.

3. Love God

This was supposed to come first in the list of people who will stand for God. Without your love for God, you will not be able to stand for Him when a situation or challenge shows up in your life. Incidentally, God

REV. DR. CHRIS OKEKE

searches our hearts to determine how much we love Him. As already said, "Jesus said If you love me, keep my commandments."

Love means intense feelings of deep affection. Loving God is a personal decision which is vital to your being accepted as one who can stand for Him. There are so many situations that will occur which demand for you to stand up for Him. In a time when people are rejecting Him and doing whatever pleases them, you oftentimes will be the only one to stand to declare Him as God Almighty. The question is: Do you really love God? If your answer is yes, then know with every assurance that you are choosing and also elected to stand for God. Here is the word of God according to Mark 12:30, "Love the Lord with all your heart and with all your soul and with all your mind and with all your strength."

4.    Love People

Loving people is one of the ways to show our love for God. There are several ways to show people that we love them.

a.    Treat and care for them as you care for yourself. Be empathetic to them.
b.    Meet their spiritual and physical needs. Share your physical resources with those who are in need.
c.    Visit them in the prison, in the hospital, or convalescent institutions. Help in their financial needs, etc. Meet their needs as much as you are able to do.

Show no partiality in your relationship with someone who does not look like you.

d.    Introduce them to the loving grace of Jesus Christ. Share the gospel and help them make a decision to follow Jesus Christ.

One of the greatest instructions Jesus gave to His disciples is to take care of His sheep. In this context, sheep means people, your neighbors inclusive, those who are spiritually dead, the world and everyone who has not known Him as Lord and Savior. Jesus called His disciples shepherds.

You and I are shepherds, we are to take care of God's people. Every disciple of Jesus Christ is a shepherd. You know, shepherds take care of the sheep. Yes, they take a lot of risks trying to protect the sheep from wild animals that try to harm them or use them as food. The shepherd is ready to die for the sheep. They will go to any level to take care of the sheep.

Taking care of the sheep is done in love, you are not to expect a reward or thank you from the sheep. You just have to take care of them with zero expectations. Jesus never billed us for His sacrificial death on the cross. He was never employed to do what He did for humanity. Jesus Christ loved us with absolute love, love without condition. That is the kind of love with which God expects us to love people.

Jesus wants His disciples to care for His people just He cares for the church. Jesus instructed them in John 21:15–17.

Jesus said to Simon Peter, "Simon, son of Jonas, Love thou me more than these?"

Peter said unto Him, "Yea, Lord; thou knowest that I love thee."

He said, "Feed my lambs."

He said to him the second time, "Simon, son of Jonas, Do you love me?"

"Yes, Lord. You know that I love You."

"Feed my sheep," Jesus told him. And he said unto him the third time, "Love thou me?"

And Peter said, "Lord, thou knowest all things; thou knowest that I love thee."

Jesus said, "Feed my sheep." John 21:15–17

An apostle is a type of the church. Jesus is saying to the church to take care of my people, the poor, the needy, the homeless, the disabled, the rich, and all people, not only those who come to the church but also those who are outside the church walls. Jesus wants you and I to share the gospel message of salvation with them so that they will also earn the free gift of eternal life.

Jesus uses the strongest words possible because of the importance He attached to saving His people. Jesus wants you to have the same attachment to love people. The scripture said how can you claim that you love God you don't see, but hate people you see. This claim does not align positively in God's eyes. So, beloved, be genuine in you approach to God. Love His people with the Love of Jesus Christ.

# STANDING FOR GOD IN CHALLENGING TIMES

Life is full of challenges. We deal with these challenges every single day of our lives; when you deal with one challenge through God's intervention, another one shows up. These problems continue until we are called home to our Creator. There is no time one can claim that he's got it all together. We are in a war, a war between good and evil, with evil trying to dominate good. Satan is the foundation of evil, he laid the foundation right from the garden of Eden. The result of his deception of Adam brought sin into the world. Since then he has been relentlessly unleashing evil into the world, because evil is the product of sin. But there is good news. Jesus died on the cross to take away our sins and restore man to holy righteousness in God.

## LIFE ISSUES

Every living persons has some kinds of life issues or crises. In this context we will define life issues as anything that is working contrary to our well-being, a troublesome situation that interferes with our everyday cycle of living.

In John 16:33 Jesus said to His disciples (including you and I), "I have told you these things so that in me you may have peace. In this world you will have tribulations." Tribulations are all the negativities you are going through, they appear in different categories as already explained above.

Yes, Jesus already informed us what to expect in the world, that is characterized with tribulations and trials, temptations of different levels, wars, etc. So, beloved, in a world filled with trouble of this sort, trusting Jesus is imperative, and the only way we can enjoy all of God's countless blessings. This question is primarily centered on how you make it for yourself, the world can be beautiful if you have Jesus Christ as Lord and Savior with whose grace and mercy we are imbued. Jesus is our peace, He is also our joy. His joy is our strength.

I tried to train my children in the word of God to be prepared for any challenges that may show up in their lives. I let them know that life is full of challenges and you well be prepared to stand strong relying Him on only and letting Him handle any situation that might show up in your life. God is always by your side to take care of you, because He loves you if you trust Him.

Life challenges or problems can come to anyone and at any time in your life. God allows these issues to come to you for different reasons;

1.  You have life's experiences
2.  You become a wiser and more strongly motivated human being
3.  It brings growth and shapes you to see the reality of life
4.  Theologically, issues and troubles of life are a sure path toward spiritual growth. The reason being that God is with you all the way. He knows what you are going through. He said in His word, "I will never leave you nor forsake you." God never lies, His word are yea and Amen.

"My troubles turned our all for the best. They forced me to learn from your textbook. Truth from your mouth means more to me than striking it rich in a gold mine." Psalm 119:1–72

Satan uses the cares of this world to de-focus the church from focusing on Jesus Christ. Issues or problems we encounter, however, can instead be used as a powerful tool to bring us back to God. God allows these circumstances and unpleasant situations to torment us day and night until we run to Him for solutions. God uses these circumstances to get our attention. James admonishes us, "When you have many kinds of troubles, you should be full of joy, because you know that these troubles test your faith and this will give you patience." James 1:2–3

Can you hear and capture the meaning to what God is saying through James? That all the issues that we are going through are for our own benefit. The moment you begin to see the pain in your life as a way up to spiritual promotion, you are heading in the right direction. Your own part is to trust in and depend on Jesus Christ.

## WALKING WITH GOD

Working with God comes with preparation. The method of this preparation is through affliction. Have you experienced affliction before?

If you are serious and want to walk with God, be ready for it! affliction is something that causes pain and suffering.

The time of our affliction is a season of another spiritual and physical promotion because God knows about it and through it your faith in God is promoted. Affliction is a time of helplessness, it is time that God is standing by you reminding you what He said in His word, "I will never leave you nor forsake you." Hebrews 14:18

God wants to walk with us. Affliction is one of the ways God brings us to walk with Him. I pray that every affliction you are going through at the moment will draw you to God so you can walk with Him.

## SPIRITUAL PROMOTION

Spiritual promotion depends on your relationship with God. God cannot start uplifting you spiritually when you don't even know Him. If you are the CEO of a company, it will be against the company's code of conduct to pull someone from the street and give him a promotion. If the person is the CEO's employee, he has to undergo some sort of training and of course know his responsibility very well before a promotion.

There is no boundary when God wants to promote you. No matter where you are, God will always fish you out and promote you spiritually. There are several reasons why God wants to promote you spiritually.

1. God wants someone He can trust to carry out His responsibilities
2. Not only trust, but someone who will be faithful (1st Corinthians 4:2)
3. Reliable
4. Dependable
5. True
6. Unfailing

All these qualities are what God is looking in a person He wants to trust. God watches and evaluates our life every second of the day. Are you faithful in the present assignment you are doing?

God wants you to bear His name anywhere you go. Listen, beloved, He called you the light of the world (Matthew 5:14), and the salt of the earth (Matthew 5:13). It was for this reason that He indwells you by His Spirit, to be a Christian who is completely engaged in the work of the Lord.

He wants us to meet the physical and spiritual needs of other people (His inheritance). In the midst of the unbelievers, He wants to be lifted up so that through you Jesus will draw all men to Himself. (John 12:32)

Spiritual promotion does not just come to you as you relax doing your thing. No, rather it comes if God found you worthy, working in His vineyard. It important to note that before any spiritual promotion, there is a test. God has to prepare you to be effective in your new spiritual position (assignment). God's test does not come with a continuous smile on your face, it is a hard experience when God allows you to go through testing which I call preparation for service. However, every test comes with His grace. His grace covers you all through the period before you attain the new position. He will allow you to go through certain unbearable conditions which sometimes, you might begin to think that you are being attacked by the devil, not knowing that it is the plan of God for your life. We can look into the life of someone who has experienced God's promotion and how they finally reached the zenith of their promotion as God designed it.

## JOSEPH: GENESIS 39

We all know the story of Joseph in the Bible. He was the last son of Jacob. Jacob was a believer of God. He fears God, so in a way you can conclude that Joseph came from a Christian family. For the most part, he came from a lineage that believed in the God of heaven and the earth. Abraham is father of Jacob, Jacob the father of Joseph. He may not have amassed himself in the word of God as a result of his young age. But, I believe that he has general knowledge of God because of the teaching he learnt at his young age under his father's tutorial.

However, Joseph faced unexpected negative events in his life when his blood brothers sold him into slavery to the Egyptians. Slavery can be defined as a restricted freedom and imposition of a forced labor on an individual. I believe Joseph faced these unbearable conditions:

Joseph's emotions were negatively affected by the sudden change of lifestyle.

Joseph missed his family, especially his father who pampered him. Jacob made him a coat of many colors.

He missed the special pampering meted to him by his father Jacob for the simple reason of the love he had for his mother Rachael. Rachael was the reason for serving Laban his uncle.

Moreover, Joseph and his brothers were the sons of their father's old age.

## JOSEPH IN THE PHARAOH'S HOUSE

Joseph was bought and brought into Pharaoh's house to be Pharaoh's slave / servant. The Scripture said, "And the Lord was with Joseph, and he was a prosperous man in the house of Pharoah." Genesis 39:2

In the same chapter, verse 3 said, "And his master saw that the Lord was with him, and that the Lord made all that he did to prosper in his hand."

From all indications you and I have seen that the Lord was with Joseph in his suffering since he left his comfort zone. The good news you and I will learn is that God is with you in your affliction and all the negativities that are bombarding you on a daily basis. I don't know what you are going through, but all you need to know is that our God does not lie, and has not changed, He is the same yesterday, today and forever. He is listening to you and will do your heart's desires according to His own way, you know God's way is always perfect.

Numbers 23:19 said, "God is not a man that He should lie, nor the son of man that He should repent, Has He said and will He not do, or has he spoken and will He not make it good."

## JOSEPH'S FAITH TESTED
## (GENESIS 39:1–END)

One of the commonest temptations which in most cases has pulled down presidents, kings, men of honor, directors and CEO's of companies, chiefs, and church leaders including senior pastors are sexual temptations. This issue seems to have a powerful entity behind it.

Every sin is serious before God, but when it comes to sexual sin, God has zero tolerance and it renders instant judgement on the offender. Our body is the temple of the living God and so He does not want His temple to be defiled.

## MOTHER'S ADVICE: PROVERBS 31

This particular chapter of the Bible talks about the advice Lemuel's mother gave to him when he was a young man. Now he has become a king and was recounting the perfect advice his mother gave to him.

The words of the king Lemuel, the prophecy that his mother taught him"

"What, my son? and what, the son of my womb? and what is the son of my vows? Give not thy strength unto women, nor thy ways to that which destroyeth kings."

Maybe you have received similar advice from your mother or your father. Every good parent prays for the success of his/her child. We all want our children to be a responsible person and successful in his/ her area of interest. Yet, do I teach such for mine?

## JOSEPH REFUSED TO GIVE IN TO SIN

The following shows the particular test that Joseph encountered while performing his duties in the king's palace. The story goes that Joseph's Master's wife wanted Joseph to lay with him. (verse 7) The Scripture states from verse 8, "But Joseph REFUSED and said to his master's wife, "Look, my master does not know what is with me in the house and he has committed all that he has to my hand.

There is no one greater in this house than I, nor has he kept back anything from me but you, because you are his wife. How then can I do this great wickedness, and SIN against God."

Verse 10, "So it was, as she spoke to Joseph day by day, that he did not heed her, to lie with her or to be with her."

Can you imagine the situation surrounding this young man? If you are placed in this kind of position or circumstances, what will you do?

## AS FOR JOSEPH,

He was honest
He was disciplined
He was a God fearing young man
He was hard working
He was obedient to his master
He had the fear of God
He was respectful

Joseph completely refused his master's wife's advance to sin. He was placed in a situation where he had to make a choice to trust God or to allow sexual sin to overtake him. It was a battle type situation. Joseph trusted God and stood solidly for Him. His actions in his master's house were a signpost through which Pharaoh's household and other people could believe in the God of the Jews. First, Pharaoh's home was blessed since Joseph entered the house. Because of Joseph's godly character, Pharaoh trusted him to the extent that Pharaoh can make Joseph his chief servant. I believe the people around were jealous of Joseph and may have even been thinking of emulating Joseph's behaviors.

The Scripture says if we find favor in the eyes of the Lord, He will make us to live and prosper in the presence of our enemies. God was with him from the very time he was brought to the house of Pharoah. Genesis 39:3 confirms that his master, the Egyptian, saw that the Lord was with Joseph and that the Lord made all that he did to prosper.

Joseph stood for God even with the intensive pressure he was going through at the hands of his master's wife to commit sin with her, but Joseph refused and instead stood for God. As a result of Joseph's determination to stand for God, he pleased God and He kept leading Joseph.

When you choose to stand for the truth of God's word, especially in a setting where everyone else turns away from it, God will honor you, because you chose to stand for Him, not for the circumstances, not for the world' standard but for God, and you are thereby acknowledging and proclaiming that He has the solution for whatever problem that is surrounding you, for God is the Truth, and Truth is God. When you choose to stand on the word of God, you are standing for the truth, for truth must always conquer. Standing for God is a rewarding experience. It breeds the peace and joy of the Lord inside of you.

Jesus Christ said, "I am the way, the truth, and the life, no one comes to the father it by me." John 14:6

## THE THREE ENTITIES OF GOD

The Way
The Truth
The Life

An entity is something with a distinct and independent existence.

## THE WAY

Jesus Christ is the only way for man's existence. He is the way to eternal life. He is the way to God. Jesus Christ is the go-between between God and man. Jesus intercedes for man. Jesus Christ took the punishment for man's sins. Jesus Christ prayed a priestly prayer for His followers according to John 17. There are no other ways to escape from death caused by Adam and Eve but through Jesus Christ. His death on the cross says it all. He is the life we live today.

## THE TRUTH

John MacArthur with radio ministry defines the Truth as; Is that which is consistent with the mind, will, character, glory, and being of God. Again he says, Truth is the self-expression of God; Jesus answered Pilate and said, "I was born for this to testify to the truth, Everyone who is of the truth listens to my voice." John 18:37

Jesus revealed His mission when He said, "I have come into the world to testify to the truth."

The Old Testament refers to God as "God of Truth." Psalm 31:5, Deuteronomy 32:4

Truth is always alive. Truth exists in the present term. When you stand for the Truth, then you definitely stand for God. Joseph solidly stood for the truth.

## THE LIFE

Life is a characteristic used to describe a living thing. The difference between the living and the dead is that a living can involve a lot of physical activities, there is an exchange of life sustaining air. A live person can breathe. A dead thing does not breathe, it does not involve any physical activities. It has no life inside of it. It is stationery with no communication. Jesus Christ is the life we live, He is our breath, His presence in us sustains us. We live because Jesus said that He has come so that we may have life and that we may have more abundantly. (John 10:10.)

1 John 5:12 declares, "whoever has the son has life, whoever does not have the son does not have life." If you don't have Jesus Christ in your life as Lord and Savior, you are spiritually dead, you are not alive. You can have the life of God inside of you by making Jesus the Lord of your life. This is the purpose of God for you, that you will know Him, the only true God. You are made in His image so that you can have His life.

As already mentioned, Joseph may have had some catechism on who God is. His father, Jacob, maybe as a "kindergarten," taught him about the story of Noah and the Ark. He must have learned that the God his father worships is powerful and can never be compared with any other. All these stories may have become embedded in his mind, so he trusted God, hence God's favor followed him even to his master's home. From the time he left his father until God uplifted him to the position of prime minister in Egypt, God never disappointed him; His favor continually followed Joseph. His purpose of being sold was accomplished in that God used him to save lives in Egypt during a devastating famine. God gave Joseph uncommon wisdom to advise his master, Pharaoh. The advice was implemented to provide for his entire family during the time of famine. God blessed Joseph and made him a blessing. God will bless you and cause you to be a blessing if you lift Him up in your daily life. God will bring every blessings promised those who obey him to pass in your life, for God is no respecter of persons, if He did for Joseph He will do the same for you and your loved ones.

## SHEDRACK, MESHACH AND ABEDNEGO (DANIEL 3)

These three Hebrew boys stood before the congregation of pagans to declare the Almighty God as the only true God who created all things. The heavens and the earth and all that existed and are existing.

They were taken as slaves when King Nebuchadnezzar invaded the City of Judah. After they arrived in Babylon, he took a special interest in the three boys; he desired that they should serve in his cabinet. You see, when the favor of God is upon you, God will cause you to live and prosper in the midst of your enemies, His favor will follow you. The favor of God was upon these three boys.

The king may have seen the talents the boys possessed. He may have been attracted by the glory of God, their God, and so he employed them to serve in his cabinet.

Babylon was a pagan country and their doctrine was centered on pagan worship of molded images of their king. They believed that their king was the ultimate, and that he was the most powerful king living.

The three Hebrew boys were innocently performing the duties of their king who they presumed to be the most powerful king living. It was in this kind of environment these Hebrew children found themselves. Daniel 1:17 said, "As for these four children, God gave them knowledge and skill in all learning and wisdom; and Daniel had understanding in all visions and dreams."

As a child of God you are endowed with a special talent, you are gifted, God expects you to serve Him with your gift. Your gift oftentimes will save you from various kinds of negative situations. God wants you to discover your gift and use it as much you have the opportunity. What is your gift? If you don't know your gift, ask God and He will reveal your gifts by the power of the Holy Spirit; only you can configure your gifts, no one else. The Holy Spirit is always available to help you.

The king had a problem which needed the attention of the astrologers. The king occasionally dreams a dream, and needs someone to interpret it. His astrologers and other wise men could not explain the dream. They all failed to meet the king's demand. These three young Hebrew boys were recommended to the king.

The people saw something very unique about these Hebrew boys. Their way of life was quite different from the Babylonian traditional lifestyle. They lived in the light of God's principles, they were quiet, they prayed to their God, and they were truthful to the king and respectful of authority. In addition, they may have had information about Daniel; i.e., how he had God's favor, and as a result the favor overflows to the king. Consequently, the king had God's favor in everything he did. So they believed that these individuals must have a solution to the king's quest.

The scripture said that God gave these children knowledge and skill in all learning and wisdom; and Daniel had understanding in all visions and dreams. (Daniel 1:17)

## THE KING'S DREAMS

No one in the land was able to interpret the king's dream, their attention was focused on the three Hebrew boys. Daniel was invited and presented the dreams for interpretation. The king and his men needed someone to interpret the king's dream. When the king is happy the people will be happy. So it becomes necessary to find an immediate solution to this troubling situation in his life.

Daniel took the dream to his friends and all agreed to present the case to God for explanation. The Bible said that God gave interpretation of the dream to Daniel, and Daniel thanked God.

The question we ought to ask ourselves is, when a situation presents itself to you, to whom do you go? For as long as there is life there will also be challenging situations that need our ultimate response. Our response to the challenge will determine how much we believe God's word. Though Daniel knew he had knowledge in skills and visions, yet he still sought the face of God. You and I should never be so confident to battle trials and temptations, but let go and let God. Our dependence on God is the key to getting problems solved. Listen, even if you think you have a solution to whatever the problem is, let the Holy Spirit be your source. Make Him your number one senior partner in all things and present your case to Him for solution. He will hear you.

## MOMENT OF DECISION
## (DANIEL 6)

Daniel's royal master Darius the Mede raised him to a very high position, he became one of the officials of the government. All Daniel's prophecies came to pass, His master's dreams which Daniel interpreted came to pass and many others which are recorded in the book. Others became envious of his position. Daniel's rivals in the government began to plot how to pull him down or even kill him in order to vacate the position. They tricked the king, Darius, making him issue a decree that for one month no one should worship any other god or man but Darius himself, and that anyone who violates his decree will be thrown into the den of lions.

Daniel's enemies knew that Daniel was devoted his God of heaven and earth. He bowed down to Jim three times a day.

In spite of this outrageous and wicked decree, Daniel continued to worship his God, giving him thanks. Daniel 6:10

Daniel demonstrated faith in action.

Faith in God drove away fear.

Daniel is our example of one who walks with God.

Daniel was reported to the king, he subsequently was arrested and thrown into the den of lion in respect of the decree the king had made. The king was distressed when he learnt that Daniel failed to keep the decree. As already mentioned, Daniel was one of the most important cabinet members in his leadership. God was with Daniel even in the den of lions. He sent his angels to close the mouth of the lions. Instead of killing Daniel, they become his friends.

## DANIEL'S TESTIMONY

The people of Medes were surprised to see Daniel alive, his enemies sorely disappointed, as they had wanted Daniel dead. The king was excited and was happy that his trusted friend was not dead after all.

When the king went to the place Daniel was thrown to check on him whether he was dead or alive, Daniel replied; "Oh king, live forever; My God hath sent His angels and hath shut the lions' mouths, that they have not hurt me; forasmuch as before Him innocence was found in me and also before thee, oh king, have I done nothing." Daniel 6:22

Daniel maintained a steadfast faith in God throughout the moment of uncertainty in his life. The king and others who served in the king's palace observed Daniel's dependence on the God of heaven. It was Daniel's faith in God that kept him through the period of temptation. Daniel stood for God even when he was threatened with death by a lion eating him up. And because he stood for God, the king and his subjects believed in God. Listen to the words of the king;

"I make a decree, That in every dominion of my kingdom, men tremble an fear before the God of Daniel; for he is the Living God, and steadfast forever, and his kingdom that which shall not be destroyed, and his dominion shall be even unto the end." Daniel 6:26

## LESSONS FROM THE LIFE OF DANIEL

1. To trust God only
2. To pray always (he prays earnestly three times a day petitioning God)
3. To forgive those who have offended you
4. To Let go and let God fix all your problems
5. Have unadulterated faith in God
6. To have patience (he went about his business)
7. Through Daniel's actions, the king and his people come to know the true God of heaven and earth. The king's proclamation to his people (Daniel l 6:26).
8. The name of the Lord was glorified

Standing for God is a tool for evangelizing all nations of the world. When you stand for God in His word, He shows up and miracles happen, then the people will see God's glory in action, they will believe Him and glorify His name.

From the life of Daniel you will discover that Daniel and his friends never shake in their faith in God. God needs individuals who can stand for Him even in the most difficult situations. God is right there with them as the particular situation evidenced. God said to prophet Joshua, "I will never leave you nor forsake you." He is ever-present in every situation you involve yourself in. Why, because He has never finished the reason He brought you to the earth. He also loves you unconditionally, He will not let any evil befall you.

God wants you to be an apologist for Him. He wants you to stand for Him. He wants to trust you, so as through you He can save His people.

## SOME FAITHFUL GIANTS WHO STOOD FOR GOD JOSHUA

There are also other servants of God in the Bible from Genesis to Revelation who stood for God in all the challenging situations that occurred. Through their unadulterated faith in God they won all the battles in which they engaged. God gave all the victories. Also, through their action other people came to know the only true God of heaven and earth.

Some of the people in the Bible whom we have an account of their faith in God are a motivational factor towards propagation of Christian faith in God. The scripture talks about Joshua the servant to Moses. Joshua was a servant whose faith in God was worth emulation.

God said to Joshua, "Every place that the sole of your foot shall upon, that have I given unto you, as I have said unto Moses." Joshua 1:3

It was because of Joshua's faith in God that God trusted him and chose him to lead the Israelites to the Promised Land. Every war and other challenges that Joshua encounters on the way, God gave victory. The power of God was so overflowing in Joshua that Joshua was engaged in one of the hottest battles between the Amorites and the Israelite Army; Joshua said to the Lord in prayer for victory over the Amorites; "O sun, stand still over Gibeon, O' moon, over the valley of Aijalon." Joshua 10:12

The scripture said, 'So the sun stood still, and the moon stopped, till the nation avenged itself on its enemies." God answered Joshua's prayer and victory was granted to the Israelites. If you believe God, God will believe in you and use you to create and recreate things. He will answer your prayers and grant you victory in the most difficult circumstances that may occur as you live on.

# MOSES
## (EXODUS 4)

Moses is one of the most pronounced prophets of God who ever lived in the history of Christianity. Humanly speaking, Moses has a definitive character of failure through his uncontrollable emotions, for example, he killed an Egyptian with the intention of trying to protect fellow Israelites. Moses broke the Ten Commandments tablet which he received from God for the Israelites, and he was angry at the behavior of the Israelites turning away from God when he went to the mountain to receive the Ten Commandments from God. When he came back, the people had already embraced idolatry. Moses initially argued with God when God called him to service. Moses' excuses, however, did not stop God from explaining to him the mode of the assignment. Moses was not prepared for this, for he looked at his handicapped side of his life. First, the scripture said that Moses was a stammerer, not eloquent in speech (Exodus 4:10)

Secondly, as Moses continued to wriggle himself out of the assignment God was giving to him, God did not relent, instead He sent his brother Aaron to accompany and help Moses on the assignment.

God never called anyone to do a thing and leave him unattended to, He will provide you with every tool you need to carry out the assignment. God removed the fear and unworthiness or self-defeat that Moses had harbored before God called Him.

Also, He promised Moses that He will be with him. Moses then had power and boldness as he set out on God's assignments.

Moses stood for God and carried out all the assignments of delivering the children of Israel from the hand of Pharaoh, the king of Egypt. Moses believed and trusted God, God trusted him and used him mightily to bring about the demonstration of His power in Egypt.

God honored Moses in the presence of Pharaoh and all the Egyptians to the extent that the people came to see Moses as god. Moses stood for God and spoke for God.

I believe that as a result of Moses' consistency in standing for God, through him God demonstrated His power and miracles before Pharaoh. I believe that through this root the people of Egypt were able to see the power of God in demonstration and as a result they came to know God.

They now believed that the power of God surpasses Pharaoh and his mighty army's power, the people now believe that Pharoah is not supreme but there's another God whose name is "**I AM THAT I AM.**" Exodus 3:14

# ELIJAH
# (1 KINGS 17)

Elijah was one of the most powerful prophets who stood for the true God of heaven and earth during the reign of King Ahab in the Northern kingdom of Israel. Then, there was the god of the Canaanites, the deity called Baal, which seemed to take the place of the true God in the hearts of the people. In other words, the people worshiped this pagan deity instead of the true God. Elijah among the other prophets evidently discussed in this book, positioned himself to save the Israelites from being corrupted by the Baal worshipers.

God wants all the people whom He called to stand out for Him and defend the gospel He gave us through Jesus Christ.

The Scripture declares, "But whoever denies me before men, him I will I also deny before my father who is in heaven." Matthew 10:33

Elijah was a radical prophet of God who challenged Ahab and his queen, Jezebel, because of the evil they committed in the presence of God because of the worship of Baal. As a result, Elijah declared catastrophic situations which will come in the form of severe drought in all the land of Israel. Ahab and his wife did not repent, instead they sought to kill Elijah. God was with Elijah and did not let Ahab's wickedness see him. In the process of time he went to face Ahab to set things right beforehand with Ahab and all the worshipers of Baal.

# MOMENT OF DECISION
# (1 KINGS 18:20–40)
# ELIJAH STOOD FOR GOD

Elijah summoned all the Baal worshipers and proposed to present themselves at Mount Carmel for a direct test of who is the true God. God of heaven or Baal / Asherah? Elijah further said, "I am only a prophet of the Lord, but Baal's prophets are 450 men and 400 Asherah worshippers.

So Ahab sent for all the Israelite and all the false prophets to gather at Mount Carmel."

Reality here shows Elijah alone standing for God competing with 850 idol worshipers of Baal and Asherah. In the context of our generation, Baal and Asherah represent anything that you place above God in your life, such things may likely be your

- job
- money
- wife
- husband
- children
- beauty
- handsome
- title
- pride

For to adequately stand for God and His cause you must place God above your needs, God must come first and all other things follow.

Consequently, many Christians still adapt to a reason why they should not learn from other radical giants of faith in God, citing as their reason, "The event was during a different time in the history of the world." Listen, beloved, this idea is one of the lined up lies from the pit of hell, it is a lie from Satan himself.

The events in the Bible are written for us to learn how the people of God apply their faith in order to please God. The word of God declared in Romans 15:4, that everything that was written in the past was written to teach us, so that through the endurance taught in the scriptures and the encouragement they provide, we might have hope. (NIV)

The false prophets will prepare their sacrifices and Elijah will also prepare his own sacrifice. Then whoever's sacrifice will be consumed by fire from his god, the same is the true God, and Him alone is to be worshipped.

The result of this show of power was that the Baal failed to consume the sacrifice by fire. Elijah called upon His God who sent fire and the sacrifice was completely consumed. When the people saw that the fire of God had consumed Elijah's sacrifice, they threw themselves on the ground and exclaimed, "The Lord is God; the Lord alone is God." 1 Kings 18:39c

Each one of us has been in a situation which can prompt us to declare our stand for God when others turned their back on Him.

Baal worshipers represent sins. Elijah destroying all the representatives of Baal is exactly how God wants us to deal with sins in our lives. God wants total eradication of sins high and low that ensnare us day and night and prevent us from living for God only.

## LESSONS FROM PROPHET ELIJAH

1.  **FAITH:** Elijah taught us how to stand in faith for God. He believed that he was the only one left and that the wicked Jezebel had killed all the prophets. Elijah knew that he was serving a living God who delivered Daniel and that He would deliver him from Ahab and his wife Jezebel. He stood alone for God. Beloved standing for God to declare Him as the only true living God. He cares for you in every situation, His concern about you is for you to do what He says, like Elijah standing in your faith, trusting, believing that what He says must come to pass, not. Minding what the world says or thinks. You are still an absolute winner when you walk in the Lord's footsteps.

2.  **BOLDNESS**

    Elijah proclaimed the word of God boldly. 2 Timothy 1:7 said that, "God has not given the spirit of fear; but of power, and of love, and of sound mind."

    Elijah never allowed fear to cripple him from obeying God. He never compromised his stand in God, even at the point when Ahab was looking for him to kill him because of the drought which seemed to have disrupted the country's economy and lifestyle of his people. Elijah never compromised his stand with God, he still followed God's commandments and was a winner, causing the generality of the people to witness the power of God in demonstration. You are victorious always when you stand for God in all your ways,

## 3. ALMIGHTY GOD

In comparison, Elijah sees God as the Almighty God of heaven and earth who is supreme in his life, who fights his wars, who provides his needs, the God of miracles and wonders, the God who answers prayers, the God who answers by fire. The only true God.

God is not, Who we can use to achieve our personal goals and drop him by the side. He is not a minute God (small god). He is not God for only one time, but an all time and all seasons God.

How do you see God? Is He truly your everyday God? The good news is that the God of Elijah is still available today. Even now, you can call on Him to reposition you so that you will honor His authority and keep His commandments. Let Him be your number one in everything you do. God called you to worship Him, let your life envelop His worship. Keep Him tuned in every day of your life, your family, in your prayers and in your family worship.

Let God be true in you. Let Jesus Christ be real in you. Let the Lord's heartbeat be your heartbeat, embrace Him daily, gossip Jesus Christ daily to your family, friends, neighborhood and everyone with whom you come in contact. Let Jesus be your business, let His concerns be your concerns. You are part of the His priests He prayed for in the book of John 17.

Again, if you are asked, Who is Jesus Christ to you, what will be your response? Your answer highly determines how you see and regard Him in your perception. Do not forget that you are part of God's family. Jesus Christ loves you and wants you to stand for Him not only in your service but in Holiness and Truth. He is your breath and life.

## 4. ELIJAH introduced the worship of the true God, called Yahweh.

The generation of the people were worshiping either Baal or Asherah as gods. Elijah believed that he was the only one left who worshiped the true God of heaven, after King Ahab and Jezebel his wife killed the other prophets.

The worship of true God was silent until Elijah showed up.

## 5.   EVANGELISM (1 Kings 18:20–24)

How long will you falter between two opinions? If God is God, follow Him, if Baal then follow him. Elijah had what I described as Holy anger, he wasted no time to declare to them the True God.

Elijah's ultimate message to the people was that there is no other supreme being but the God of Heaven and Earth, the God of Israel whose name is Yahweh.

The people understood Elijah's introduction of who the true God is, hence they uniformly shouted, "The Lord, He is God, The Lord, He is God!" after they saw the power of God in demonstration. 1 Kings 18:39

I believe the events at Mount Carmel must have continued to resonate in their minds, which may eventually have led them to total commitment in serving the true God of Heaven and Earth. I believe we all have witnessed the power of God in demonstration in our lives or in our family or friends. Our perception of who God is has given us enough evidence to trust God and declare, "He is God! He is God!"

Drawing people to Jesus Christ is the fundamental reason for you to stand for God. When you stand for God, your main focus should be that the people watching or the people standing by you should see the presence and power of God in demonstration. We are called to evangelize the world, those who have not received Jesus Christ as their personal Lord and Savior. Yes, Elijah stood for God even when other people followed the other gods. Elijah lifted the name of his God high, and as a result, the people's attention was drawn to God. John 12:32 declares, "And I, when I am lifted up from the earth, I will draw all men to myself.'

Friend, God elected you before you were born to be the limelight through which the world will see the worthiness of the omnipotent God in creation. This you do through obedience to all His commandments, no matter what the world says or does, you undoubtedly stand for Him.

## 6.   PROPHET EZEKIEL

Ezekiel was one of the central priests and prophets in ancient Israel. He was the author of the book of Ezekiel. He was exiled in Babylon where God called him to take His message to His people. Ezekiel's prophecy to the people was a message of hope for the restoration of His people. He was one of the four major prophets who does not compromise his faith in the God of heaven. Prophet Ezekiel solidly stood for the cause of God, he never shivered when it comes to delivering God's messages.

In Chapter 37, Ezekiel saw the vision of two dry bones which symbolizes the restoration of Israel. And He said unto me, "Son of man, can these bones live? And I answered, oh Lord thou knowest. And He said unto me, Prophesy upon these bones, and say unto them, O ye dry bones, hear the word of the Lord, Thus saint the Lord unto these bones; I will cause breath to enter into you and you shall live; And I will lay sinews upon you and will bring up flesh upon you and cover you with skin, and put breath in you and he shall know that I am the Lord." Ezekiel 37:3–6

Ezekiel sees sins as man's impediment to the knowledge of God, hence he preaches judgement on sin, he believes and instructs on personal accountability when it come sins.

"The soul that sinneth, it shall die. The son shall not bear the iniquity of the father, neither shall the father bear the iniquity of the son. The righteousness of the righteous shall be upon him, and the wickedness of the wicked shall be upon him." Ezekiel 18:20–24

God is willing to deliver His people from any form of bondage. Each time God stretches out His righteousness to rescue those in bondage, sins seem to stand in the way. "All have sinned and fall short of the glory of God." Romans 3:23

You are called to the office of a prophet, your ultimate responsibility is to stand for God in your calling, God has a message for His people, the message goes to them through you, therefore God requires your total attention. He requires your participation in building or participating in populating the kingdom of God.

Apostle John commanded, "But, If we confess our sins, He is faithful and just to forgive us our sins and cleanse us from all unrighteousness." 1 John 1:9

It was for the sin of humanity that Jesus died on the cross that we might be free. You and I are free if we receive Christ in our life as Lord and Savior.

Our belief in God and our personal conduct should be the central focus of every follower of God, to make sure that our conduct is in line with God's commandments.

God is interested in every detail of our lives. If we claim to be God's children, then it is our responsibility to walk in the part that does not counteract our faith and worship of Him. He deserves all our worship. He does not like competition with any other entities we might be putting our faith in. Rather, He prefers a mind that seeks Him in love and in holiness.

Analytically, it was because of these entities known as Baal and Asherah in the lives of the people of Israel that Prophet Elijah declared before his audience seeking a decision between Baal and Asherah worshipers, and for them to make a choice now, "if Baal is god, worship him, if God is God, then worship Him," he challenged them.

God went further to speak to His people through Prophet Ezekiel; "And I sought for a man among them, that should make the hedge, and stand in the gap before me for the land that I should not destroy, but found none.

Therefore, have I poured out mine indignation upon them; I have consumed them with the fire of my wrath: their own way have I recommenced upon their heads, saith the Lord God." Ezekiel 22:30–31

CHAPTER 7

# God Os Looking For You

As we have already discussed, God seeks for a man who will stand for Him so that through him He radiates the light of His countenance on the world of darkness. Are you that man/woman? Can He trust you to be that vessel? Does your faith in God come by believing that Jesus is the only Son of God who shed His precious blood for the remission of your sins? If this is your story, then you are absolutely the man God is looking for. The prophets and priests in the Bible who stood for God chose to stand out for God while others stood as nominal believers.

God is not looking for nominal Christians, but those with solid faith in Him.

Secondly, God is looking for those who will partake in His divine nature. His divine nature meaning we are godly. We have His nature.

You and I are made and called to be part of God's family, that is why He gave us His nature. We are made in His image. Genesis 1:26a declares, "Come, let us make man in our own image."

Every good father loves his son, especially when he looks like him in every aspect, walks and talks like him. People usually say "he is a carbon copy of his dad." You will probably love him so much that you refer to him as the extension of God's love to you and the family. Beloved, the love you have for your children can never be compared with the love that God has for you. He loves you everlastingly, meaning till eternity. There is nothing you can do that will ever cut short His love for you, even when you sin He is still loves you, but does not love the sin in you. It was because of His love that He sent His only begotten Son Jesus Christ to die on the cross to save you and have you by His side. Do you sometimes feel His presence and love on you?

God did not love you theoretically, but in demonstration of His love (practical), the scripture said, "But God demonstrated His love towards us in that while we were yet sinners, Christ died for us." Romans 5:8

Standing for God in all your actions is the ultimate reason He elected you. Are you standing for God? If your answer is no, then where are you?

## SEARCH THE BIBLE

As already stated, the Old Testament and the New Testament sections of the Bible both record men and women who stood for God in all circumstances. This day and time, we study their giant strides in faith, we even study about their books, we study more about them and their relation with God in the Bible colleges and Theological institutions of learning. They choose to do only what God said and what pleases Him, and as a result God trusts them and demonstrates His power through them. These servants of God were blessed in so many ways. We read and study what they did to be recognized by God.

Abraham was another man of faith in the Bible who is worth emulating. It was because of his unadulterated faith in God that God called him His friend. He was known and called the father of faith.

## GOD TESTED ABRAHAM'S FAITH

Genesis 22:2 recorded God's specific instructions to Abraham to offer a burnt sacrifice to the Lord. Burnt is an offering burned on the altar as a religious sacrifice. He said to Abraham as recorded in the Scripture quoted above, "Take your son, your only son whom you loved-Isaac and go to the region of Moriah. Sacrifice him there as a burnt offering on a mountain I will show you." Since you come to the Lord through Jesus Christ, have you heard a specific instruction from God directing you do certain things for Him? I believe He has spoken to you over some issues about yourself or someone else. Yes, He speaks to His children most times, even as you read this book. The ultimate question is, are you listening? It is absolutely necessary for a child of God to learn the voice of the Father. The joy of the Lord comes when He knows that you understand and follow His commandments.

Abraham had every reason to talk himself out of what God said. He did not follow his emotions; rather he decided to follow the inner still voice of the Holy Spirit and do what he believed God was saying.

It is important to note that Abraham knows when God is saying something to Him. He can identify God's voice from any other voice. After all, he had several encounters with God, at least in the issue of his son Isaac. He had Isaac when he had lost hope of ever having a child.

When no human science can affect the bearing of a child, God intervened and they had Isaac. Consequently, Abraham pleaded for his cousin Lot to be spared when Sodom and Gomorrah were about to be destroyed as a result of sins.

The same God who had mercy on them now asked Abraham to sacrifice the same Isaac on Mount Moriah. He never questioned God's decision. He understood that God is merciful and will always make a way out of no way. He must have reasoned that God had an alternative so He decided to follow God's instructions to sacrifice Isaac.

Can you imagine yourself in place of Abraham, we all know the story of Abraham. His wife Sarah was barren for many years until God opened her womb at an age when the desire and hope had already gone, and God was the God of impossibility who made a way where there's no way, and Sarah became pregnant and Isaac was the result. My friend, no matter what you are going through, you may have been written off by people, but you have good news. God can make impossibilities in your life possible so that you can praise Him. He can turn things around for you for free.

There was great joy in the household of Abraham. God brought great joy to Abraham and his family. This single unexpected miracle gave Abraham hope and assurance that he now had a son who would inherit his great possessions. God is no respecter of persons, He can do a similar thing for you and your family. The Scripture says with God all things are possible. He never changes or alters in His ways.

Now the same God who gave Abraham a son was the same God who asked Abraham to sacrifice the same son. For you and I, we would most likely believe that the instruction is not from God, we may start fasting and praying, binding and loosing, not knowing that the test was from God.

I do think that Abraham binding his own son was more hurtful to Abraham than he could have hurt his son Isaac. Abraham's faith in God may have assured him of God's providential capacity, in a way God will provide a lamb for the sacrifice. In the focal point of slaughtering Isaac, God stopped him and provided him with a lamb.

This singular act of obedience brought Abraham into the limelight of God's faithful servants. God trusted Abraham and called him "His friend," or friend of God. James 2:23 says, "Abraham believed God, and because of his faith, God accepted him as righteous And so Abraham was called a friend of God."

God never does anything without revealing it to His friend Abraham.

## LESSONS ON ABRAHAM

### 1. OBEDIENCE:

Obedience is compliance with an order or request or law, it also means submission to another's authority.

Abraham is one of the best examples of those who truly obeyed God's voice. They carried out the instructions God gave to them without a single alteration. His obedience earned him the name a "Friend of God," and in addition God changed his name from Abram to Abraham. In the name Abraham were blessings embedded.

If you choose to obey God today, your blessings will begin to unfold right before your eyes. When you obey God in His words, He is obligated to reach you with all that He has for you. In every situation, first enquire from God what He will have you do. I am pretty sure that God will definitely speak. Abraham did not hesitate to take his son for the sacrifice. He obeyed God's voice.

## 2.  FAITH

Abraham is known as the Father of Faith. He had unshakable faith in God, his faith focused on the facts about God. He believed that God will provide something for the sacrifice. Abraham had the spiritual discipline to trust God anyhow no matter what the situation looked like. Abraham's record of God's faithfulness in his life had been the bridge though which his faith was catapulted to him been called the "FATHER OF FAITH" (Romans 4:16) and ("FRIEND OF GOD") James 2:23

The Bible records, "But without faith it is impossible to please Him, for he that cometh to God must believe that he is, and that he is a rewarder of them that diligently seek Him." Hebrews 11:6

Faith is a complete trust or confidence in God. So, beloved of God, to stand for God, we need absolute unadulterated faith in Him. Romans 10:17 says, "Faith comes by hearing, hearing by the word of God."

You and I need faith to be able to understand who God is and how to follow Him. To access and build up our faith requires us to go back to the Bible daily. After you access the word of God, then you must put it into practice. The scripture says "faith without work is dead." A dead faith is something that has no value. We must practice to obey God, if you fail initially, confess to God and continue to practice obedience. Dealing with a part of a relationship requires continuity, so if you fail at first, retreat, look where you failed, and do it again after you have prayed for God's leading you to obey Him. Our God encourages forwardness in His service. He does not encourage backwardness. He has no time for laziness and complainers.

David in the Bible failed when he committed adultery with Bathsheba and murdered her husband in the process of trying to cover up his sins. One lovely thing about David is that when David realized his mistakes, he repented, got up, asked for forgiveness and moved on serving the Lord and fighting the Lord's battles.

When you find out that you have sinned or that you did not follow God's commandments, repent, do not sit and have pity party, go on and serve the Lord. God will always forgive anyone who repents from their sins. Yes, our God is very kind and merciful, He never followed us according to our iniquity, but is always ready to forgive us from all our sins.

## 3.   TRUST

In order to have the fullness of God you must trust Him, knowing that He is God. He wants us to trust Him is all circumstances so as to rescue us from every ugly situation we may have found ourselves. In difficult situations, trust Him, while we go through hardship, trust Him. God never failed anyone before. If we find that things are not going well in our lives, retreat, go to Him in prayer and ask Him to help you to overcome such situations. I am pretty sure that He will, and will give you a fresh beginning. Do not take God for granted, go back to the Bible, read and study the Bible daily, then practice to live out whatever it says.

Joshua trusted Him to defeat the enemies of Israel. He did, and it was because of Joshua standing for God that he was able to command the sun to stand still and the moon to stand while he slaughtered the enemies of Israel. Something like this never happened in the history of man. God can use you to demonstrate His power in any situation that calls for it if you trust Him.

Elijah stood for God and trusted Him to send fire to consume the sacrifice at Mount Moriah when Elijah challenged the prophets of Baal and the Asherah worshipers. God answered and the people believed in Him after they saw that He was the true God, not Baal. If you stand for God, He will draw others to Himself.

Abraham trusted Him for a child, He gave him Isaac.

My question is, what are you trusting God for? Whatever it is, He is able and abundantly able to meet your needs.

We are always to:

> Stand in obedience
> Stand in faith.
> Trust Him
> Do not doubt
> Then His presence will be abundant for you
> God speaking, "am the Lord, I change not." Malachi 3:6

## APOSTLE PAUL

Paul was one of the outstanding apostles in the New Testament of the Bible who stood for God the things of God.

You and I will remember that Paul, formerly known as Saul was a leading person that antagonized and persecuted the church to the extent that he killed and put those who escaped death in prison. The church obviously knew about Saul and his wicked acts against the worshipers of God, he literally created fear among the worshipers of God who were alive and are not in prison. The Scripture says that he got permission from the High Priest to put in jail those Christians he will arrest.

In confidence like other times, Paul was on a mission to arrest more Christians and was walking on the dusty road close to Damascus when the Lord met him. The Bible recorded that a bright light shone on his face and he became instantly blind and fell onto the ground. While he was still on the ground confused by what was going on, the Lord asked him one of the most crucial questions which I believe applies to us as well, "SAUL, SAUL, WHY DO YOU PERSECUTE ME?" Acts 9:4

Paul's dramatic experience brought about a total turning point in Paul's whole life:

- From persecutor of the church to the builder of the church
- From faithless to faithful
- From Hate to Love
- From unbelief to belief

God uses any means He chooses to call us to ministry. We all differ in the ways God calls each and every one of us to serve. My experience may be different from your experience. For Paul, his turning point was with a hard lesson associated with blindness and total stripping of his ego and confidence that he had in himself and those who supported him.

Paul was led into the city where Ananias the priest prayed and laid hands on him in the name of Jesus Christ to receive his sight.

In the process of time Paul grew to become one of the most outstanding faith builders in the New Testament of the Bible. He followed Jesus Christ and did an outstanding job preaching and leading people to

Salvation in Christ. In all his suffering and persecution which he went through, Paul never turned away from following Jesus Christ. He suffered uncountable persecutions and a lot of near death situations including the shipwreck in Acts 27, but Paul never backed out of his faith in the Lord. Instead, Paul used every affliction and suffering which he was going through to preach the Salvation message to his audience and to assure them of Jesus' willingness to save the people. In all, Paul stood to lift the name of Jesus Christ above whatever odds they were going through.

Paul was powerfully anointed because of his obedience to the word of God. The word of was so alive in Paul that he utilized the authority in the name of Jesus Christ to get the devil off from afflicted people who attended his crusades. Through Apostle Paul, the blind received their sight, and the lame walked.

Anointing on Paul's handkerchief was used to heal a person. Apostle Paul obeyed God's word and followed Him without any kind of alterations. Paul was so confident in the Lord that his slogan and one of his encouraging words was "TO LIVE IS CHRIST BUT TO DIE IS GAIN." Philippians 1:21

This book is all about standing for God at all times. Paul in all his sufferings still stood solidly for God and continued to obey what God said. He did not move because of the immediate circumstances that afflicted him. He was not moved by pity partying criers or the world's greatest philosophers, rather he was moved by the word of God. Paul kept moving forward in the knowledge of the word of God. There was no iota of doubt in his relationship and honoring of Jesus Christ. He was so confident and focused doing the will of God.

## LESSONS FROM APOSTLE PAUL

### 1. God can change you.

Before Paul had his encounter with Jesus, he can be categorized as a murderer, a hater, disgruntled and a misguided elitist. God did not look at Paul's failures, however, but instead bestowed His grace upon him. The grace of God says even though you are a sinner, I forgive you. Grace is therefore known as unmerited favor of God. If it were to be you and I, we would have written Paul off our mind. We would have formed an opinion of him and put him in a certain level of individuals who does not need any good thing in life. But thank God for His grace, which is still available to us and to them who discover it.

God does not think the way we think. "For my thoughts are not your thoughts, neither are your ways my ways," declares the Lord," Isaiah 55:8

If God can use someone like Paul, He can also use you and I; no matter the kind of lifestyle or grievous things we have done, He can use us to fulfill His purpose on the earth. Do not try to put yourself down as a result of your past. Jesus has already paid for those sins at the cross. You need not hold unto it anymore. You are free from past sins, as well as present and future sins. However, every sin you commit repeatedly after Jesus has forgiven you which are not confessed carry some consequences.

God is watching you after you repented and surrender your life to the Lordship of Jesus Christ. The word of God says that sins committed in ignorance are forgiven, having been washed away by the blood of Jesus. So, therefore, sins you committed after you confessed Jesus Christ as your Lord and Savior have some consequences. It is like crucifying Jesus Christ on the cross for the second time. God does not deal with fools.

Thomas Fuller, a theologian in the past century said; many has been the wise speeches of fools, though not so many as the foolish speeches of wise men."

The Scripture talks about fools in the book of Proverbs. It says the way of fools is right in their own eyes. Proverbs 12:15

Whenever we know what is right before the Lord and we choose instead to do what we know is wrong, the Bible calls such a person a fool. As already said, there are some consequences for willingly sinning against God, unless we repent of it. We are to form a habit to practice sinless actions. Any time we do sin, confess it right away and practice not to do the same thing again.

Thankfully, God is interested in how we are living for Him now, today, not yesterday. Yesterday's sins have been dealt with, they are gone.

## DO NOT LET YOUR PAST DEFINE YOU

Every one of us has a past lifestyle of sins. In a religious context, according to an online definition of sin, sit is a transgression against divine law. Literally, the definition of sin differs from culture to culture. In general terms, sin can be defined as doing something or saying something against the proscribed ethical structure. And it is recognized and carries some consequences in the ways in which we have lived or are still living. This past is compounded by the sins of Adam and Eve and it is offensive before God. I would like to emphasize that your past may be yesterday or an hour ago or yesterday's back.

## THE WHOLE DUTY OF MAN

Let us hear the conclusion of the whole matter, "Fear God and keep His commandments, for this is the whole duty of man." Ecclesiastes 12:13

Theologically, fear in this context means reverence, respect, and honor. God is good. He loves us so much and will not create us to fear Him, rather He loves us and wants a reciprocal love from us. If we are to honor and obey Him, however, there should be some measure of fear for Him.

## 1.  LOVE GOD

We are so used to talking of God's love for us. We have all experienced His love in diverse ways. No one could ever deny the fact that he had not seen the genuineness of God's love and His faithfulness in His promises to us. The Scriptures declare that God is love, and His personality and everything about Him is love. His breath is love, His touch is love. His love is poured out on man. We will be in serious error if we don't identify His love for us both in personal and collective ways. You may have had some experience of rejection from someone you love and may have trusted, but as you were in this condition you felt the presence of the Holy Spirit whispering saying it is well, I am with you. The word of God declares, "I will never leave you nor forsake you. Beloved, God is with you 24/7, God is with you:

as you sleep and wake
as you walk
as you work
as you sit on the dining table and eat
as you are with your friends.
in the church
Doing evangelism and other forms of worship.

God is with you to bless you, and through you He will draw all men to Himself. He is everywhere you are to protect and help you go through the daily challenges of this life.

God knows you before you were born. "Before I formed you in the womb, I knew you and before you were born I consecrated you, I appointed you prophets to the nations." Jeremiah 1:5

Beloved, this a powerful statement about you, if God had not loved you, He wouldn't have prepared you even before you were born. Every move of God on you and me is compounded in His love. He strides further into loving us by becoming man in order to fulfill the purpose He had for humanity, that is to solve the sin problem. It will be obviously right if at some points you will note down proofs of God's love for you. If this is done to you, perhaps you can see beyond what physical eyes can see why you should love God.

Some time ago, I asked a gentleman we were ministering the love of Jesus to, and I asked him, "Do you know that God loves you?"

He said, "Yes I know."

Then I asked again, don't love God? He was quick to say yes, and I said good, then I asked him, "How do you know that you love God?" You see, a lot of people do not know why they should love God. If you are in this group of people, the points illuminated below may give you a guide to see the many reasons why you should love Him.

## I LOVE GOD BECAUSE:

- He gave me eternal life in Him through the death and resurrection of His only begotten Son, Jesus Christ

- He kept me alive to see this day, and experience His blessings
- He provides all my needs and my family's needs
- He delivers me from our enemies
- He gives me peace in chaotic situations
- He fights all my battles
- I experience His mercy and grace every day
- He forgives all my sins
- He keeps me focused on Him; even when I wander away in sin, He brings me back to Him

## KEEP HIS COMMANDMENTS

God wants us to keep all His commandments as written in the Bible. This is one of the ways God determines our love for Him. We have often failed in this direction and it is attributed to us as sin against Him, the only way to get of it is through confession. 1 John 1:9 says, "if we confess our sins, He is faithful and just to forgive us our sins and to cleanse us from all unrighteousness."

To love God is a command. The book of Luke stated it this way; "One of Jesus' audience asked Him, What must I do to inherit eternal life?

And Jesus answered, "Love the Lord your God with all your heart and with all your soul and with all your strength and with all your mind and love your neighbor as well." Luke 10:25–28

Again Jesus spoke to the people in the book of John; "If you love me, keep my commandments, And I will pray the father, and he shall give you another comforter, that he may abide with you forever, even the Spirit of truth whom the world cannot receive because it sees him not, neither knoweth him, but ye know him, for he dwelleth with you and shall be in you. I will not leave you comfortless, I will come to you." John 14:15–18

Basically, if you decide to stand for God, you are actually not standing by yourself, His Holy Spirit is right there with you. Let me inform you, in every facet of your service to the Lord, the Lord is right there with you. To help you live for Him, He gives you His Spirit.

## THE GRACE OF GOD

The Grace of God helps us to:

- Have faith In Him
- Believe Him in His word
- Forgive those who have offended you, including your enemies
- Do your job in your office with a godly heart
- Be a good manager
- Be an achiever
- Seek positively on the things that will please God
- Ask God for His grace during temptations so that you can go out into the world without being consumed in it
- Live life for Him on a daily basis and bring us into another day.

Did you witness the grace of God in your life or members of your family recently? Grace simply means unmerited favor. We are not supposed to be where we are today, but His grace has brought us to where we are.

His grace sustains the universe. His grace has lifted us up in a position of high authority where we are at the moment. If you are not seeing the grace of God at the moment, then reach out and receive it now for it is always available to whoever seeks Him. The Bible says that God is not a respecter of persons. Ask God to guide you with His grace in everything that you are doing no matter how small or how big, and His grace will give you success. In my family, we always conclude our prayers with grace to guide us for the day. Paul stated it like this" "May the grace of our Lord Jesus Christ and the love of God and the fellowship of the Holy Spirit be with you now and forever more. Amen." 2 Corinthians 13:14

We never end our prayers without saying the grace of God. His grace is alive and well. May God's grace be your potion in this season in the name of Jesus Christ.

As already stated, obeying God's commandments is a sure way to tell God you love Him.

Him with all your heart, spirit and soul. When you do this, He will send His Comforter, the Holy Spirit to indwell you forever! {What a glorious life.} His Spirit will help you to grow in your spiritual life from glory to glory.

## LOVE PEOPLE

Another similar commandment is to love people, not only in word but in actions. Yes, beloved, love can be demonstrated, this is done by meeting the physical and spiritual needs of people. Jesus demonstrated His love while we are still sinners (Romans 5:8).

When you meet the needs of people, you are definitely touching the heart of God, and He is pleased with you. To reach out to the people was the reason Jesus Christ came. Jesus came and spent all His life on earth doing good to people. While John was still in prison, he heard Jesus' fame was all over the city. He sent his disciples to Jesus and said, He therefore required us to continue to do His ministry while He was away. We are to give account of our stewardship when He comes back.

## YOUR NEIGHBOR EXPLAINED
## (LUKE 10:25)

When you think about who your neighbor is, usually our minds race to the people living at the next house close to you, or someone you share the neighborhood with, or some other people living in the same apartments. Those are also our neighbors but Jesus explained to us who our neighbors are in Luke 10:25. Jesus told a story of a certain man who journeyed to Jericho, and was attacked by armed bandits, who stripped him half dead, and by chance there came down a certain priest that way; and when he saw him he passed by on the other side.

But a certain Samaritan, as he passing came where he was and when he saw him he had compassion on him and went to him and bound his wounds, pouring in oil and wine, and set him on his own beast, and brought him to an inn and took care of him.

Not only did this Samaritan take the wounded man to the hospital but he also paid the hospital bills. Jesus got the people to understand that your neighbor can be anybody, it may not necessarily be your household member or your tribe, but any person. Therefore, we should see anyone as a neighbor, whether such a person is white or black, and it does not matter where the person comes from, God wants us to see people as He sees them. He sees you and I, and the whole world with the eyes of compassion. We should deal with each other as we deal with ourselves. Jesus commanded us to love our neighbor as ourselves.

If we fail in this commandment, it is attributed to us as sin.

## ACCOUNTABILITY

We stand accountable to the work committed to us. "For we must all appear before the judgment seat of Christ." 2 Corinthians 5:10 (for believers in Christ alone).

Those who do not have Christ as Lord and Savior will also be judged for refusing to receive the offer of salvation which God gave to man in Jesus Christ.

Assuming you were to die today and stand before God and He were to ask you why should I let you into my heaven, what will you say? Or alternatively, What did you do with Jesus Christ?

Jesus Christ will be coming back to the earth anytime. Will you be ready? Will I be ready?

We are to strive daily to stand for God and the things of God so that He will draw all men unto Himself.

## MAKE DISCIPLES

A disciple is someone who follows his master. We are called to make disciples of all nations. We are not just called to live like a Christian but also, we are called to make disciples of all nations. The Bible recorded that immediately after Jesus was baptized, He went from village to village to village preaching the kingdom of God and people turning from their sins and believing the gospel. The first sermon as written in the Bible says, "Repent, for the kingdom of God is at Hand" (Matthew 4:17). The book of Mark also recorded the same first sermon from the Lord Himself.

1. You are to receive Jesus Christ by faith in your life as Lord and savior Romans 10:9

2. You must study your Bible daily 2 Timothy 2:15
3. You must share the testimony of conversion to overcome the devil Rev. 12:11
4. You must pray without ceasing 1 Thessalonians 5:16–18
5. You must fellowship with the other believers (the church) Hebrews 10:25.
6. You must apply what you learn from the Bible and let it rule your life every day John 14:15
7. You must allow the Holy Spirit to lead you as you go into your daily orientations Psalm 103:10. He is a person, talk to Him and be honest.

## JOHN THE BAPTIST

John was one of the people God elected to stand for Him. The first page of the book of John introduces him as a man sent from God. It went ahead to shed light on the mission of John on earth. The Scripture revealed that he came to give testimony, to testify about the light so that all might believe through him. John 1:6–7

Incidentally, the ministry of John is the same ministry we are called to do. The responsibility given to the church is a package in which every member of the body of Christ has a share in it. You pick up your own area and I pick up my own area, and the result of each area we choose is a common goal which is eternal life in Christ. Everything we do for the Lord must be something that attracts unbelievers to eternity in heaven. Therefore, as you stand to lift the name of Jesus Christ, He will draw all men to Himself.

The book of John is one of the best books in the Bible which gives us a deep knowledge of who Christ is and what He came to do. Paul unfolded the love of God for humanity, and how to be saved for eternity. John was a typical example of how the New Testament worshipers should stand for God. John was radical in his faith in God.

The religious leaders saw the light of God shining through him as he baptized those who come to know Jesus Christ in the river Jordan. The news went round the town guessing whether John was Jesus who they were expecting at the time. The people saw something different in John, he was not like the other preacher. So the Jews sent a message through the priests to investigate if John is the Jesus they are expecting? The question they throw to John was, "Who are you? So we can take the answer you gave to the people who sent us." The Scripture reported that John simply answered, "I am the voice of one crying out, make a straight road in the desert for the Lord—Just as the prophet Isaiah said." John 1:23

# CHAPTER 8

# Elected for God

When God chooses you, He will also elect you to a specific office of assignment. God elected you because He trusts you to stand in faith and glorify His name even in the midst of the unbelievers. He trust you to propagate the kingdom of God by sharing the gospel and in other forms of obedience to Him.

As already discussed above, standing for God is in a different dimension. You can stand for God physically, this means more actions such as going to share the gospel and dancing to the glory of God, through the arts. The word of God sums it up this way, in 2 Corinthians 8:12, "For if the willingness is there, the gift is acceptable according to what one has, not according to what he does not have." (see Jean E., art as worship.)

You can also stand for God spiritually. This refers to meditation, prayer, and counseling Godly wisdom. Of course, in every forms of worship the Holy Spirit must be involved, worshiping God without the leading of the Holy Spirit renders the service powerless. The Holy Spirit is the motivating factor. He accompanied you for a physical service, He indwells you and I for service that pleases God. As already said, without the Holy Spirit our service will be more of flash that quickly disappears.

The Scripture says that God is a Spirit and those who worship Him must worship Him in Spirit and in truth. Yes, both actions of standing for God are led by His Spirit. Both actions point to the glory of God, and those you come in contact with will see God in you, this is because you are indwelled by His Spirit. One of the main works of the Hoy Spirit is to enable you live a godly life to His glory. You will not be moved by any prevailing situations, because you are standing for Him.

Your election is not by accident. It was predetermined before you were born. Jeremiah 1:5 says, "Before I formed thee in the belly I knew thee; and before thou comest forth out of the womb I sanctified thee, a prophet unto the nations."

One of the responsibility that awaits every believer of Jesus Christ is to discover your assigned responsibility. Such a responsibility is what God wants you to stand for to lift up the name the name of Jesus high so that others can see and seek Him. What is your assigned responsibility? If someone asks you today, what area of the ministry of Jesus Christ are you serving, what would be your answer?

I have served the Lord in the evangelism ministry over 27 years as of today, and I am still serving to the glory of God. We go to the streets and door to door informing people how much God loves them and that God is willing to give them eternal life if any one of them will invite Him into his life as their personal Lord and Savior. We pray for people if necessary if the Holy Spirit leads us, we encourage people who have invited the Lord into their life as their Lord and Savior to pray and study their Bible daily. We give them room to ask questions as well.

## EQUIPPED FOR GOD

When God elevates you to stand for Him, He also equips you for the service of reconciliation of the role to Himself. Apostle Paul explains it this way, "And all things are of God, who hath reconciled us to Himself by Jesus Christ, and hath given to us the ministry of reconciliation; To wit, that God was in reconciling the world unto Himself not imputing their trespasses unto them and hath committed to unto us the word of reconciliation." 2 Corinthians 5:18–19

He declared, "I will never leave you nor forsake you." Your election for the service of God starts immediately when you make Jesus Christ your Lord and Savior, you become a child of God. Every child of God is a soldier of the cross, you are enlisted as part of the armies of heaven serving as an ambassador for Jesus here in the planet earth.

2 Timothy 2:4 said, "No man that warreth entangle himself with the affairs of this life; that he may please him who hath chosen him to be a soldier." One of the characteristics of a soldier is to follow the commands of the superior officer. He does not entangle himself in other affairs, if he does he may lose focus of his responsibility. You know God does not want us to lose our focus on Him, that is why He put a strong word to this effect that we should keep looking upon Jesus Christ was has brought us this far.

"Looking unto Jesus, the author and finisher of our faith, who for the joy that was set before Him endured the cross, despising the shame, and is set down at the right hand of the throne of God." Hebrews 12:2

Look unto Jesus Christ by;

a.   Reading and studying the word of God day and night
b.   Obedience to His word as written in the Bible
c.   Meeting the needs of other people
d.   Participating in kingdom building
e.   Fellowshipping with other believers

If we can be serious about observing the above laid down principles, God will be pleased with us and will trust us to reveal more of His awesome personality as well.

## LET GOD BE YOUR RESERVOIR

Any child of God who wishes to stand for God must make God the reservoir of his life. A reservoir is a natural or artificial lake used as a source of water supply. A reservoir can be constructed or it can be one which is naturally placed by God. The central function of a reservoir is to hold some quantity of water for use. It may be managed by a community of people or an individual. In either case, it holds some quantity of water which is released to the people as needed.

God is the reservoir of our lives. He created us in His image, He gave us life, He protected us, He watches over us, He heals our sicknesses, He provides for our needs. Above all He gave us eternal life In-Him. If you are alive today, it is because of God's mercies. Lamentations 3:22 says, "It is of the Lord's mercies that we are not consumed because His compassion fails not, they are new every morning, great is thy faithfulness."

Therefore, beloved, is God the reservoir of your life? If your answer is no, then the good news is that you still have hope now, today. Make Jesus Christ the Lord of your life and stand for God in His word and you will see the glory of God in action.

If God is the reservoir of your life then you can be sure that you will have the supply of anything you need if you obey and trust Him. Such things you need which will glorify His name. When you feel spiritual dryness, which we all do at some point in our walk with Him, He will be right there to refresh you and give you a new beginning.

In addition His grace, which is very much available, will supply all your needs in Christ Jesus. Ask God for His grace to be able to do such a thing for all you want and all that you want to do. (God, I need your grace to be able to live for You daily)

Remember that inside God's reservoir (grace) you have life, power, anointing, obedience, righteous life, goodness, mercy and fullness of God.

As already stated, you can get anything you want by the grace of God. If you stand for God through Jesus Christ, His grace will be available to you at all times, in season and out of season, of your life. God wants all those who trust Him as their personal Lord and Savior to look to Him for everything. Are you being harassed by your boss, tell it to God. Are you in conflict with someone, talk to God. Do you have a court case, take it to God. Are you denied of your right, take it to God. Are you looking for a promotion, take it to God. Whatever the situation you are going through, God wants you to present it to Him. You can report your spouse to God if he/she is misbehaving.

The reason we run into problems is the fact that we try to solve the particular issues we have on our own, or taking the advice of our friends who even reject Christ as their Lord and personal Savior.

Here is a song that reminds us how we completely depend on God to deal with our issues.

LEAVE IT THERE, LEAVE IT THERE
TAKE YOUR PROBLEMS TO THE LORD, LEAVE IT THERE

HE WILL SURLELY DELIVER YOU IF YOU PUT YOUR
TRUST IN HIM
TAKE YOUR PROBLEMS TO THE LORD, LEAVE IT THERE.

This song tells it all. God is a problem solver, if you choose to stand for Him in faith doing what He says in the Bible, then He will be obligated to give you undivided attention. Standing for the Lord also tells the element of TRUST you have for Him. You cannot say you stand for God if you don't trust Him, correspondingly you cannot say you trust Him if you don't stand for Him in faith. Trust is one of the key elements that motivates you to stand for Him. Trusting Him depends on how much time you spend with Him in His words, the Bible, for the more you study the Bible is the more your faith is developed. The scripture said, "Faith comes by hearing, hearing by the word of God." Romans 10:17

## GOD LISTENS TO YOU

If you carefully go through the pages of the Bible from Genesis to Revelation, you will discover that those who stood in faith for God got His attention. They asked God questions, correspondingly, God gave the answer, and they followed whatever He said resulting in getting victory to whatever they were requesting from Him. Remember in the Old Testament, when God was about to destroy the city of Sodom and Gomorrah, Abraham pleaded with God to spare the innocent residents of the city. God answered Abraham that if there is a certain number of righteous people He will spare the city from destruction. Genesis 14

God talked with Moses when He was about to deliver the children of Israel from their bondage in Egypt. There was such a beautiful communication between Moses and God. Moses followed God's instruction word for word and the result was total deliverance of the children of Israel from Egypt (Exodus).

God will hear you when you talk to Him. In fact, one of the reasons Jesus Christ came into our world was to open up communication between us and God. God needs you to tell Him every detail of your life. He wants to know what is troubling you at every point of your life. God is no respecter of persons, so this is the same for each one of us Acts 10:34

If He can give attention to others who have run the race before you, He can also give attention to you for whatever you are presenting to Him.

You are made His image. Have you ever thought of the fact that you are God's image. Image in this context means that you and I are exact spiritual replicas of God. Again, the Scripture says that we are in His likeness.

I will obviously discuss the word "likeness" separately. The Holy Spirit who indwells us constantly reveals to our spirit that we are God's image, and He loves us so much. Did you get the revelation of whose image you are, or did you just read it in the Bible and let it go? I would like to mention to you that you will attain a high level of assurance of your faith in Jesus Christ if you discover your person in Him. You can only benefit from Him if you know for sure that you are in His image. A lot of brothers and sisters do not have the knowledge of whom they represent. It is your responsibility to know Him in a personal way. God is waiting and watching, He still loves you unconditionally.

Genesis 1:26–27 is one of the greatest Bible passages which assures us of who we exactly are. And God said, "let us make man in our image, after our likeness and let them have dominion over the fish of the sea, and the fowl of the air and over the cattle and over every creeping thing that crepe that upon the earth." It says, "So God created man in His own image; in the image of God He created him; male and female created he them."

God made us best of all His creations. He created us different from all other ones. We are a special species, just like Him. I am so happy that I am in His image. God loves us beyond measure, we are loved unconditionally. 1 John 3:1 declared, "What manner of love the Lord had on us that we should be called the child of God…"

Not only are we in His image, we are also in His likeness, there is a slight difference between image and likeness.

## "IN HIS LIKENESS"

LIKENESS talks about God's qualities, His characteristics or attributes. Yes, we have some of God's qualities, we are in His likeness, this means, if Jesus Christ can heal the sick, you can as well heal a sick person. If He can raise a dead person, you too can heal a dead person.

You and I are special to God, He created us unique and gave us all of His qualities so we can care for His inheritance. Yes, He created us to be able to care for His other creations. He gave us intelligence to create and recreate things. Lions, cobras and other creations hear your commands and obey.

After God created us and loved us, He gave every other of His creations' charge concerning us;

### "Touch Not My Anointed, and Do My Prophet No Harm"
### Psalm 105:15

It was because you are in His likeness that He placed you to be in charge of all His creations and gave you a special place in Him. The only way to recognize this responsibility is your absolute faith in Him. Faith is has been the only formula to see who God is. Faith catapults your spiritual life to a level of moving the mountain. Jesus speaking through Matthew 17:20 told us that if you have a tiny faith as tiny as a mustard seed that you can move a mountain from one place to the other. A mountain in this context represents problems of all types:

- Blindness
- Cancer
- Poverty
- Lack
- Death
- Marital problems and other forms of family issues

There are other forms of afflictions that trouble us on a daily basis. These issues make our lives very unpleasant. But, some of these are for our good, it is for our spiritual growth, which may result in searching for the living God. When you are stretched by any form of affliction you are going through and you find that there is no help from man, you will probably start looking for God. For a believer in the Lord Jesus Christ, afflictions are intended to increase your growth in the knowledge of God. As you go through the difficult time, God is with you all through the period of the affliction.

Psalm 23:4 says, "Yea, though I walk through the valley of the shadow of death, I will fear no evil; for you are with me; your rod and your staff, they comfort me."

Jesus assured His followers with these comforting words. He said, "I have overcome the world" and its problems. This assurance is for those who have made Him their Lord and Savior. In essence, we have every right to command every troubling situation to stop in the name of Jesus Christ. Yes, beloved, we have the power and anointing to subject everything the way we want it to operate. When we speak or command in the name of Jesus Christ it will obey and God will receive all the glory. When situations hear the name of Jesus Christ, they simply obey.

"For in the name of Jesus Christ every knee bows and every tongue confess that Jesus Christ is Lord." How long ago has it been since you invoked the name of Jesus Christ over your troubling situation, or are you just praying for God to take it away?

Your faith in God is your license to pull down every strong problem that presents itself to you or your family. God's intention says that if you stand in faith for Him, believing, then you can command all these problems to stop and they will stop immediately. The songwriter says,

### "If You Run to God, God Will Run to You"

Can you at this moment imagine the quality of a person that you and I are made of. You are obviously endued with power and anointing beyond measure. No creation can do what you and I can do. Jesus made the blind see, we can make the blind see.

In the book of Acts chapter 3:1–7, Peter and Paul were going to the mid-week Bible study when a blind man at the beautiful gate asked for alms (money) from people entering the place of worship. They asked Paul and Peter to give him some arms (money). They replied to the blind man, "Silver and gold have we none, but what we have I give to you (emphasis is mine) and they issued a command;

"In the name of Jesus Christ of Nazareth, rise up and walk."

168

As a believer in Jesus Christ, the most valuable property in your life is the name of "JESUS CHRIST." The name of Jesus Christ is what made you a Christian. It is the name that gives you Authority to do unimaginable things which no other creatures can do. It is a name that can stand any storm of life.

We wear the name Jesus Christ like clothes and it goes wherever we go. Not only do we wear the name, but the name indwells us. John 14:20 says, "On that day you will realize that I am in my father, and you are in me and I am in you."

The name of the Lord is a strong tower, the righteous runs in and he is saved. Proverbs 18:10

Beloved of God, standing for God and taking action in the name of our Lord Jesus Christ in the area of our needs is what this book is all about. Whenever you stand for God, the heavenly host stands solidly with you to bring to pass whatever thing that you are praying for. When you issue a command, according to the word of God it will be done according to your request. Peter and Paul issued a command to the mountain of cripple which bound a man sitting at the beautiful gate. The demons behind the cripple obeyed their command and the cripple was able to see and the glory went to the Lord. The man lived a joyful life the rest of his life just as the Lord intended before he was born.

## STANDING FOR GOD REQUIRES COMMITMENT

The online definition of this topic says, "it is the engagement of obligation that restricts freedom of action." Biblically, it means engaging in the Lord's work without distractions from other sources. Yes, for you to really stand for God requires two entities:

### 1.   SPIRITUAL COMMITMENT (FAITH)

This term talks about your Faith in the Lord. Faith is Spiritual. Faith is the evidence of things hoped for, the appearance of things not seen. Hebrews 11:1

Faith is not in the physical form, this means that you cannot touch it or feel it, but you can see what it does. Faith leads to action and action produces physical result. Are you believing the Lord for anything? If yes is your answer, then direct your faith on Jesus Christ, not on the substance (problem). Abraham's faith in God resulted in the birth of Isaac.

The Scripture again said, without faith it is impossible to please God.

Therefore, Faith in the Lord Jesus Christ is one of the Spiritual symbols of a true Christian. Are you a Christian? If you are, what is the measure of your faith? How do you weigh yourself? As already discussed above, you are to stand for God in your faith.

When trials and other forms of affliction show up in your life, then the only effective weapon to fight such a trial is your faith in Jesus Christ. Your faith in His promises for you, your faith that the battle belongs to Him. Your faith that He had given you victory over such issues with which you are struggling. Your faith that what He said He will do and that He is going to do it.

Your faith in God causes God to give you special attention and meet your needs faster than you expected. Consequently, your faith in God remains the easy access to the throne room of His grace. In the throne room of His Grace, everything you need is easily obtainable. While other Christians are fasting and praying and going for retreat, because of your unadulterated faith and obedience to His commandments, your case becomes different.

Prophet Samuel said to King Saul, "Hath the Lord as great delight in burnt offering and sacrifices as in obeying the voice of the Lord? Behold to obey is better than sacrifice and to harken than the fat of a ram." 1 Samuel 15:22.

Prophet Samuel was one of the powerful prophets in the Old Testament whose faith (spiritual) was in God, but he was also a man of action (works)

No matter the situation which you are going through, or other faith challenges, you must see your faith telling you to continue to trust Him until what you are believing in Him is evidenced. If for any reason you fail in building it up or you feel that you are spiritually dried up or that the Holy Spirit who you talk to seems not to be around anymore, then present your feelings to Him and ask Him to help you focus again to please Him.

For your faith to continue in its upward growth, you must practice what I call faith exercise. In other words, practice using faith in everything you do. As already said, you practice keeping faith. Get up and continue if you fail.

In addition to the relative miracles which you have seen Him do, you are to practice believing in Him for small things like having faith that God will provide you a spot to park your car where there are parking challenges. However before you practice faith in Him, you must daily purify yourself by confessing your sins and repenting from them. You are to stand righteous before Him daily.

## 2.  PHYSICAL COMMITMENT

This term describes the practical ways in which you employ to serve the Lord. Every promise of God to you needs your participation to bring what you requested to manifestation. When you pray in faith over a particular thing you need, God immediately answers you, all you need to do is to fulfill your own part is twofold

1.   Ask.
2.   Action (physical)

To receive your request, your physical participation is needed to bring the answers to your requests.

Elijah prayed in faith, God answered by fire and consumed the sacrifices. First of all, Elijah prepared the altar, then God sent the fire and the sacrifice was completely consumed. As already explained, faith calls in works, then the answer is achieved.

Faith without works is dead (James 2:14). Yes, for you to be active in serving the Lord and standing for Him, your faith and works (action) must be combined together. The book of James tried to explain it this way, "For as the body without the Spirit is dead, so faith without works is dead also." James 2:26

Physical aspects of your service to the Lord cannot survive the Biblical definition of works, if it is not produced from faith action. Also, faith cannot be what it is if it is not backed up by works. That is why faith without work is dead, but work without faith is dead also, period. We are to render our service to the Lord making sure that both faith and works are in the

171

state of combined equilibrium. When faith and work are combined, the Holy Spirit produces in you the joy of service.

This is why Christians who understand these principles are fearless, even when the most difficult situation shows up as they are working for the Lord, they endure even if losing one's life is involved, this is so because of their decision to stand for the Lord. Consequently, they stood solidly without fear or discouragement, they are not afraid to die for the sake of Christ. Paul declared: "To live is Christ, and to die is gain." Philippians 1:21

Literally, you will constantly experience the inner joy of the Holy Spirit as you continue to stand for Him in faith. Moreso, you will overflow with the anointing of the Holy Spirit. In addition, because you stood for Him, He will use you to accomplish some things which had proved impossible before other people and other means.

You can lay your hands on the sick and he will recover immediately. Lame, blind etc., will recover when you lay your hands. In the book of Acts of the Apostles, handkerchiefs from the Apostle Paul was taken to a sick person and when it is placed on him, he recovers from sickness. Elijah, Elisha, Joshua, and other men of God operated under this anointing and got results. Anointing of God from Evangelist Katherine Coleman throws people down when they pass close to the building where she was ministering.

God can work through you if only you can obey and stand for Him in faith. You and I are not different in God's perspective, He loves us equally. He will use us if we are available in faith for Him. If you carefully meditate in the word of God, you will discover God's delight in you and His intention to position you so He can move you to the next level of faith so that you can be the light He made you to be. God is interested in you. He made you a unique individual and endowed you with special talent.

Again, you can start building up by going to Him through His only begotten Son, Jesus Christ, yes, He is the only way to build up your spiritual muscle of faith, no other way! Then go to the word of God consistently and practice standing for God in a time of adversity

## PANDEMIC

The word "pandemic" is an epidemic of some sort of disease which has the capacity to spread over a large geographical area.

Adversity simply means difficulties; misfortune. The term represents a whole bunch of problems or ugly situations which undermine the ethical systems of living which was ordained by God from the beginning of creation. Adversity may be in what I call hardship or health issues. Whatever the unpleasant situations that derails our peace and joy can be adversity.

This book is written in a time when the whole world was besieged with a type of disease known as COVID19 or Corona Virus. According to the news, the disease originated from Wuhan, China, since March 2019 and until today, 7/17/20, thousands of people have died as a result of the virus and millions are diagnosed positive for the virus. All the hospitals were overfilled with people who tested positive for the virus and the mortuaries are overfilled with corpses of people who have died from the virus. Worse still, the government has not come out with any proven care, and no vaccine or **medicine seems to cure or prevent the virus.**

The economies of most nations are negatively affected, and many companies closed down, All schools were closed. Churches and other spiritual places of worship were also closed. People are instructed by the government to stay home. Travel in and outside the countries are banned. Wearing face masks is enforced in all countries of the world.

People hope and wait for things to change. Christians prayed and trust God for His intervention.

# CHAPTER 9

# The Meaning of the Church

A lot of people do not know the true meaning of the church, yet they go to the church every Sunday and attend after the church activities as well. As we embrace this discussion of the true meaning of the church and its responsibilities, open your heart and let the Holy Spirit witness some truth about the church into your Spirit.

First of all, the Church is a collection of people of the same faith in worship of their God. Secondly the church can be defined as, a collection of those who have invited Jesus Christ into their life as Lord and Savior by faith and who have the hope of eternal life in Him.

Churches are people not buildings, Jesus is always in the church to receive all the glory and praise accorded to Him. Jesus said, "when two or three are gathered in my name I am there in their midst." Matthew 18:20

It is absolutely necessary to begin to teach our children and our Bible students that the church is not a physical structure of a building. The church is a collection of God's people with one faith in the Lord Jesus Christ. That God is always available in the church (two or more people) to bless His children.

There are diverse creative miracles in a cooperate worship in the church. I went to visit a close relative sometime ago. A mere looking at him told me that he did not go the service that morning, so I asked him, did you go to the church? He told me that he had a church online, meaning that he watched preachers on the television. There are super anointings on you that breaks every yoke and heal every manner of diseases when children come together in worship. Each time you come to the church with expectation, God meets you and lift that burden off you so you go home not the way you came. Every time we come before God and fail to receive from Him, the blame should be on us and not God. He has already positioned all of His children who trust Him, to have faith and obey to receive whatever He wants.

"Therefore I tell you, whatever you ask for in prayer, believe you have received it, and it will be yours." Mark 11:24

## THE CHURCH IS THE BODY OF CHRIST

Ephesians 1:22–23 says, "And He put all things under His feet, and gave Him to be head over all things to the church, Which is His body, the fullness of Him who fills all in all."

The Scripture said that Christ is before all things and in Him all things hold together and He is the head of the church (Colossians 1:17–18).

Analogically, Paul uses the relationship of husband and wife to describe Jesus' teaching as head of the church. "Wives, submit yourselves to your own husband as you do to the Lord, for the husband is the head of the wife as Christ is the head of the church, His body of which He is the Savior." Ephesians 5:22

There is no church without Jesus Christ, just as the scripture said, He is the head of the church, the church is the body of Christ. If we cut off the head then the body will not survive. As a body, Christ takes care of the body making sure that it is physically fit to carry the head. Jesus takes care of us emotionally, physically and spiritually. Why not become part of the body of Jesus Christ? If you are not part of the body, do it now by inviting Him to be you Lord and Savior. He will surely answer you.

175

# THE CHURCH'S RESPONSIBILITIES

The church is a physical structure were people of the same faith gather together to worship. It may be a private or public place. The Greek word for the church is ekklesia, meaning congregation or assembly. Jesus Christ Himself founded the church. T Matthew in his writing quoting Jesus Christ, said, "And I also said to you, thou at Peter And on this rock I will build my church and the gate of hell shall not prevail against it." Matthew 16:18

The above statement is a powerful and direct statement from the Lord Jesus Christ. You see, different governments past and present have been trying to do away with Church. Even in your community, a lot of people may have wished that the church does not exist. They prosecute and in prison Christians who proclaimed the gospel of our Lord and Savior Jesus Christ. Till this day the church is still waxing strong despite the wave of persecution against Christians going on in many nations of the world. However, God wants His followers to keep focusing on the assignments of spreading the gospel all over the world.

## MINISTRY GIFTS

The scripture says in Acts 4:11, He Himself gave some to be,

    Apostles
    Prophets
    Pastors
    Evangelists
    Teachers

Ephesians 4:11–12, in verse 12, says, "for the equipping of the saints for the work of the ministry." As already mentioned, God categorized these gifts for us to be effective carrying out our calling in the most effective ways.

Whatever talent you have, it is for the work of God, nothing more added. Yes, they are pulled together to take care of God's responsibility which is His inheritance, the people.

Church Responsibilities:

1.   LOVE GOD. This is the first responsibility God I trusted to the church, to love Him.

One of the ways to love God is to keep His commandments.
Jesus said, "if you love me, keep my commandments." John 14:15

2.   LOVE PEOPLE.

Another church responsibility is to love people. "My commandment is this, love each other as I l have loved you. Greater love has no one than this; to lay down one's life for one's friends." John 15:12–13

3.   SHARING CHRIST.

Evangelism is another essential responsibility for the church. Listen, God gave the church a mandate to take the gospel outside the church building to the streets, byways and highways. cities, towns and other vicinities. He said specifically, to the church, "Go into all the world and preach the gospel to every creature." Mark 16:15

The people that you are ministering to are God's inheritance, by sharing the gospel, you are giving them opportunity for hope of eternal life in Christ Jesus.

4.   AKING A DISCIPLES.

This is another major responsibility for the church. It is the responsibility of the church to help new converts to grow spiritually to maturity, that is, to become disciples of Jesus Christ. Arc you a disciple? It pleases God that all the people in the church will grow to maturity and become a disciple of Jesus Christ. (A DISCIPLE IS ONE WHO FOLLOWS JESUS CHRIST)

After one gave his or her life to the Lord according to Romans 10:9, if you confess with your mouth the Lord Jesus Christ and believe in your heart that God has raised Him from death, you will be saved.

Following this confession of faith, the church still have the responsibility to bring this individual to maturity through follow up:

Discipleship
Bible study participation

Getting involved in other church activities aimed at sharing Christ and making disciples.

The church is equipped and mandated to help people to be effective in his / her calling. Are you faithful in your calling, or are you simply in a group that "plays church?" Which side are you on?

## WHAT IT MEANS TO BE BORN AGAIN

Born again is a phrase used when one repents from his sins and invites Jesus Christ by faith into his life as Lord and Savior. This refers to a new birth in Christ. Our first birth was in sin through Adam's sin orchestrated by Satan. We are all born in sin, no one is righteous, no one. We are the offspring Adam and Eve. Even as an infant we came into this world with sin in us, we had the sin nature in us because it runs through our blood. No wonder David in confessing his sin said, "Surely I was sinful at birth, sinful from the time my mother conceived me, yet you desired faithfulness in the womb; you taught me wisdom in that secret place." Psalm 51:5 (NIV)

So therefore, beloved, part of God's requirement is that we have a new life in His Son, Jesus Christ and new ways in His righteousness. The second birth is spiritual, which guarantees our eternal life in Jesus Christ. This condition was what Jesus Christ was trying to explain to Nicodemus in the book of John. Jesus said to Nicodemus, a member of the Jewish ruling council, "You must be born again."

The Scripture puts it this way, "Very truly I tell you no one can see the kingdom of God unless they are born again." John 3:3 (NIV)

Nicodemus got confused and further asked, "How can someone be born when they are old?" Nicodemus asked, "Surely they cannot enter a second time into their mother's womb to be born." John 3:4

Jesus replied, "Very truly I tell you no one can enter the kingdom of God unless they are born of water and the Spirit." John 3:5

These two items, water and Spirit, though they differ in our own understanding, but both of them do the same thing: purification and sanctification for eternal life in Christ. We are to discuss these two elements further in this topic as we go on. I would like to chip in, the essence which Jesus was trying to inform Nicodemus that a complete turnaround in his life is needed to be born again. Turning around means repentance from the sin of Adam to the righteousness of God in His Son Jesus Christ, and turning away from his sins. Turning around means turning away 180 degrees from your sins, and never to visit your old life of sins again.

## BORN OF WATER AND SPIRIT MEANING

First of all, water is a good thing, water is used in all life's circle. Water is part of a component that keeps a child in the womb alive until the circle of pregnancy is completed. Water is used for spiritual cleansing. Specifically in the Old Testament, figuratively water is used for spiritual cleansing. The book of Ezekiel says, "I will sprinkle clean water on you, and you will be clean, I will clean you from all your impurities and from all your idols." Ezekiel 36:25

In our everyday lives we need water to survive. The importance of water in the lives of people can never be over emphasized, that is why Jesus said to Nicodemus "You must be born of water." The ignorance of Nicodemus over Jesus' sentence of being "born again" made Jesus Christ to do incidental teaching on Nicodemus to clear all doubt clouding Nicodemus' mind and help him to understand who Jesus truly is.

## BORN OF THE SPIRIT SPEAKS OF SPIRITUAL BIRTH

This talks of eternal life in Jesus Christ. When you are born of the Spirit of God, He releases His Spirit inside of you and His works start immediately according to John:14 26. Jesus said to His disciples, "The Holy Spirit, whom the father will send in my name, He will teach you all things and bring to your remembrance all that I have said to you." Yes, the Spirit convicts you of the cross and brings the cross and its significant to your understanding so you can believe that Jesus actually died on the cross and was resurrected on the third day. He will expose the nature of God to you and help you in your faith walk.

He will give you the assurance of your salvation and boldness to obey and proclaim the gospel. He will provide wise counsel to you. In general. it is important to note that when the Holy Spirit indwells you, all the characteristics of God will become evident in your life. What you did wrong before you came to Christ you will do more, even if you want to do them it will become impossible because the Spirit of God is now the CEO of your life. I was drinking before I came to Christ, but how I stopped drinking only God knows; every form of alcoholic beverage became my enemy to the extent that whenever I even smell it, I become uncomfortable until I leave the scene. Moreso, your life will be transformed to the image of God with astronomical growth to His glory. When you undergo these experiences of transformation, know that God is getting you ready for your assignment. Be ready to stand for the Lord wherever you find yourself. Amen.

## YOU ARE THE TEMPLE OF THE HOLY SPIRIT

"Do you not know that you are the temple of the Holy Spirit and that the Holy Spirit dwells in you?" 1 Corinthians 3:16

The Holy Spirit of God brings a dramatic change in you and changes the way you see and do things. He changes your actions and your utterances to reflect the one you are representing whose name is Jesus Christ.

In the book of Acts, believers in the Lord Jesus had a similar experience, they lived in obedience by following the footsteps of Jesus. The people who are not even Christians observed the way they do things, and immediately discovered a sharp difference in the way they lived and acted and the way they followed Jesus Christ, how they lived and acted; after they observed these changes they discovered what they had seen in others, their statements confirmed what they were thinking:

"THEY ARE CHRIST LIKE!"

As you surrender yourself to stand for Christ, they are watching you every day to determine if you will falter in your newfound life. So, as you stand for God, infuse yourself in the Holy Spirit, let Him envelop you at all times, as you carry out your assignments.

When you are born again by inviting Jesus into your life as your Lord and personal Savior, His blood cleanses you from your sins, and the Holy Spirit comes to indwell you. One of the reasons He indwells you is to teach you to live a life of holiness. The things you do before, you do them no more, the places you go before, you go there no more. Your life will be completely transformed. You will begin to live a godly lifestyle, a Christlike lifestyle. The lifestyle you lead at the time after you received Christ into your life is orchestrated by the Holy Spirit not you. However, this new life in Christ starts as you study the Bible and do what it says in obedience to God.

As a Christian, it is absolutely important to know that you are indwelled by the Holy Spirit, moreover, that you believe and agree with Him in His word, the Bible.

Those who are born of Spirit and water live the life of obedience to God. We must listen to the voice of the Holy Spirit and must be led by Him if we want to please God. Do you want to live for God? Do you want to enjoy your Christian lifestyle ? Do you want to be led by the Spirit of God, acknowledging His presence in your life? Apostle Paul confirms this when he said to his audience, "For those who are led by the Spirit of God are the children of God." Romans 8:14

The mark of a child of God is the unique characteristics of the Holy Spirit seen in you. After you made Jesus the Lord of your life, God released His spirit to indwell you and continue to teach and reveal the mind of God to you. God will begin to speak clearly as you read and study the Bible.

## OBJECTIVE WORK OF THE HOLY SPIRIT IN A BELIEVER

"Nevertheless, I tell you the truth, it is expedient for you, that I go away for if I go not away the comforter will not come unto you, but if I depart, I will send him unto you and when he come he will reprove of the world of sin and of righteousness and of Judgement of sin because I go to my father and you see me, no more of judgement because the prince of this world is judged." John 16:7–11

1.  Counselor
2.  Advocate
3.  Teacher
4.  Intercessor
5.  Helper
6.  Strengthener
7.  Comforter
8.  Conviction of Sin.
9.  Sanctifies-
10. Testifies-

Your spiritual growth depends on your commitment and acceptance of Him in your life. His holy influence on the body of Christ sanctifies you and every congregant in a worship service.

One who is not indwelled by the Holy Spirit may not experience His power to set free and the joy and peace through His indwelling of His Spirit. It is always a good practice to check and ask the Holy Spirit any question that you may have. Yes, He is available to give answers to our questions and concerns.

## REASON JESUS CHRIST CAME TO THE EARTH

The purpose of Jesus Christ coming to earth has always been for one reason: to save us from our sin, and restore our relationship with God, our Father. Our relationship was broken as a result of the sin of Adam. The sin of Adam stands in our way of receiving our blessing from God, but Jesus stepped in to set us free through His sacrificial death on the cross.

God' love for humanity was one of the central issues that prompted His coming to save the sinners. The grace and mercy of God is obviously available to lead the sinner from the channel of death to the channel of life in Christ Jesus. Ultimately, God demands that we must be born again in order to have a new nature which is still available to those who come to Him in faith. The two words that characterize a true born again Christian are Spirit and water. Jesus said you must be born of Spirit and water.

Baptism of the Holy Spirit gives the authority and empowerment of Jesus as a true believer of Christ. The Spirit is the presence of God in you, being the authority required to stand against every negative influence attempting to interfere with the work of God in you. While water baptism points to public declaration of identity in

1. Believe that you are a sinner.

Romans 3:23

The word of God says that if we deny that we have not sinned we make God a liar, Apostle John puts it this way, "If we claim to be without sin, we deceive ourselves and the truth is not in us." 1 John 1:8

"If we claim that we have not sinned, we make Him out to be a liar and his word is not in us/" 1 John 1:10

## GOD WILL FORGIVE YOUR SINS

John 1:9 says, "If we confess our sins, He is faithful and just and will forgive us our sins and purify us from all unrighteousness." We must agree that we have all sinned, we are to repent and confess our sins according to the Scripture.

If you repent from your sins and confess them according to the word of God, He will in turn forgive you. Then you are to invite Him into your life as your personal Lord and Savior according to the pattern in the book of Romans, which says, "If you confess with your mouth the Lord Jesus Christ and believe in your heart that God has raised Him from the dead you will be saved." Romans 10:9

If you willingly invite Jesus into your heart to be your Lord and Savior, the Bible says this of you: "you will be saved."

Salvation of our soul is the highest form of CHRISTIAN benefit. Yes, knowing the Lord alone is good, but a relationship with Jesus is what it takes to earn God's favor.

The message of salvation is the message of love of God for the sinner. God said "I love you" (John 3:16). In addition, He said, I will demonstrate My love to you. He demonstrated His love by letting His only begotten Son, Jesus Christ to go through the most humiliating moment in the history of the world, then crucified on the cross of Calvary where He died with your sin and mine hanging on Him. The scripture says He died, and then rose again after been in the grave for three solid days.

Have you ever experienced humiliation? Humiliation is publicly injuring someone's feelings. Humiliation hurts, it causes one to feel dejected and unwanted by anyone. Jesus took the humiliation for us. Jesus' decision to die for us gives us life and confidence to face life's issues, especially if you have known Him as Lord and your personal Savior. Jesus will give you the meaning to life, His blood deletes your past life of sins and give you eternal life of glory in Him.

God thinks more about you than any other of His creatures and will never stop loving you, He hears you when you speak to, Him He meets you at every point of your needs. God will never stop thinking about you, He says your name is written in His own very arms.

He meant everything He said in His word about you and will bring it to pass. Jesus said I will never leave you nor forsake you. Yes, beloved, Jesus is with you even when you go through trials and other kinds of hardships. In His grace. God stretched His hands to welcome you to life in Him through His son Jesus Christ. It is important to note that for man to be saved, he needs His Son. In His Son is the fullness of God. Yes, everything about God is in His Son. As already said, if you have His Son, you have life, if you do not have His Son, you do not have life.

The Scripture said, "And this is the testimony: that God has given us eternal life, and this life is in His son. He who has the son has life, he who does not have the son of God does not have life." 1 John 5:11–12 (NKJV)

Ultimately, when you have Jesus Christ in your life, you automatically have the fullness of God in you,.

Have you invited Jesus Christ into your life as your personal Lord and Savior? Do it now!

## DOES A GOOD PERSON NEED SALVATION?

There has been a lot of controversy around this view: "Does a good man need salvation." Psalm 14:3 says, "There is none who does good, not even one." A simple definition of a good man is one who is careful in dealing with others (online definition of a good man). In a different denomination today, people present themselves and believe that they are good persons.

Our evaluation of a good person portrays him as someone who is dedicated in the service of the Lord (Theology). Such a person comes to the church every Sunday. He is a friend of the senior pastor and even listed as one of the prominent persons in and outside the congregation of God's people.

He gives alms and helps needy persons. These individuals are what our society has tagged "good" but the Scripture already declared that no one is good. We all have sinned before the Almighty God. We all are born in sin.

A lot of people are confident that based on a "good person syndrome" they have already attained what it takes to go to heaven. In the book of John Chapter 3, the Scripture talks about Nicodemus, a Jewish leader, a statesman and a man of the people who gives alms and cares for the people. Nicodemus thought he was all set to be among those who will enter heaven. When he heard Jesus teaching, he got convicted and wanted to hear more about the message and the miracles Jesus performed, which to him serves as evidence of the fact that Jesus Christ came from God. He wanted to know more about Jesus. Scripture said that he went to Jesus by night and asked Him, saying, "Rabbi, we know that you are a teacher come from God, for no one can do these signs that you do unless God is with him.

You see, Nicodemus in sincerity of his heart needed clarification.

Jesus answered, "Most assuredly, I say to you unless one is born again he cannot see the kingdom of God."

The fact applicable to everyone in the church is "YOU MUST BE BORN AGAIN." One must receive Jesus Christ into his life by faith. Yes, God recognizes your deeds, kindness and other charitable acts performed. They are still not standard for eternal life in Christ Jesus. God has only one standard and that is by His grace. Ephesians 2:8–9 declares, "For by grace you have been saved through faith, and that not of yourselves; it is the gift of God, not of works, lest anyone should boast."

It is only through God's grace that we have eternal life, not what we do. Only through Jesus Christ can we earn eternal life.

In the book of Acts, it said, "Neither is there salvation in any other: for there is no other name under heaven given among men whereby we must be saved." Acts 4:12

We are in before God meets us where we are and picks us up by His grace and mercy. Apostle Paul said, "But God demonstrated His own love in that while we still sinners Christ died for us." Roman 5:8

God finished His work for us, it is a one-time atonement, which means in union with God through Jesus Christ's sacrifice at the cross. We are supposed to jubilate at all times for what Jesus did in our lives. Beloved, the grace is still available even now!

## CHRIST'S DEATH AND RESURRECTION: HOW WE PARTICIPATE THROUGH BAPTISM (ROMANS 6:3–4)

A lot of believers in the church do not know the significance of baptism. Baptism means unity with God, yes, we are united to God through the sacrificial death of Jesus Christ on the cross. Through Baptism we are endowed with His power and presence for service. Jesus brought us into unity with the Father. Once in a while our pastors will announce that those who have received Jesus as personal Lord and Savior and who wish to be baptized sign up for this ceremony. It is important to know what Baptism means before you sign up. First, you must have repented from your sins and have made Jesus Christ your personal Lord and Savior.

These issues must be settled in your life before baptism:

First, the scripture says that we are all sinners. Roman 3:23 tells us, "All have sinned and fall short of the glory of God." Read it again, "ALL," not some but all. You have sinned, I have sinned, and the whole world has equally sinned against our Holy God. Ultimately, this is the only reason God sent His only Son to the world to deliver us from physical and eternal death. He shed His innocence for us, in order for us to live.

So, to be born again you must participate in the death of Jesus Christ on the cross by making Jesus Christ your Lord and personal Savior.

Furthermore, Romans 10:9 says that if you confess with your mouth the Lord Jesus Christ and believe in your heart that God has raised Him from the dead you will be save, in essence if you,

1. Believe that you are a sinner
2. Repent from your sins, confess them before the Lord, and turn your back on them
3. Invite Jesus Christ into your life as your personal Lord and Savior

## WHAT'S NEXT?

Do everything necessary to grow in your newfound faith, specifically depending on the Holy Spirit in your daily orientations, reading, and attending Christian crusades. God does not want you to be a stationary believer, but a believer who grows spiritually in the knowledge of the word of God. Faith cometh by hearing, hearing by the word of God. Romans 10:17

Find a Bible Believing Church and be faithful in your participation.

Keep all the commandments of God as stated in the Bible, let God know your struggles and your weaknesses, see God your only first responder, as there will be emergencies in your life or that of loved ones. God never fails anyone, remember He is with you anywhere and anytime.

Share your faith with others who have not heard of the gospel. (evangelize)

Be faithful and consistent in your service to Him.

If you serve the Lord faithfully, God will lift you up spiritually to the next level of service in Him.

Here are some statements about a good man:

"A good man leaves in hesitance for his children." Proverb 7:24a

"For there is not just a man on earth who does good and does not sin." Ecclesiastes 7:20.

## WATCH AND PRAY
## (MATTHEW 26:41)

"Watch and pray that ye enter not into temptation."

Watching and praying should be our decoration as a minister of God. Prayer is simply a communication between you and God. Prayer should not be a seasonal event, rather it should be something that we do at all times. In time of trouble and in the time of peace. If possible, while you are awake or while you are asleep, while you are driving or while you are walking, while you are sitting or while you are standing, in good times and in bad times. Beloved, make prayer part of your everyday lifestyle.

Prayer is the key to every successful ministry. No congregations can succeed in their quest for God without fervent prayers. A prayer-less congregation is a powerless congregation. I would like to list five powerful elements about prayer:

> Prayer draws us to God
> Prayer creates love in us towards other people
> Prayer creates in us a new heart every time we pray
> Prayer touches the heart of God and He releases His mercy upon us
> Prayer goes far beyond our geographical location, you can pray for a person in India and God will answer and do what you prayed for. Or a person in Russia, or the Middle East or in Nigeria, Africa.

God answers you according to His promises in His word, therefore, pray from His word reminding Him what He said. God has never failed anyone who prayed according to His word.

Prayer is so important that Jesus commanded us to pray without ceasing.

Don Gibson, speaking, said, "prayer is the key and faith unlocks the door to heaven."

If you want to be successful standing for God in righteousness, in trust, in obedience and in belief, then you must be a Christian who prays without season.

Sometime ago, I was listening to an interview granted to Pastor David Yoggi Cho, a popular South Korean pastor who pastors the largest congregations of people in the world, about 830,000 members, on asking how he is managing such large congregations all over the world. Pastor Yoggi Sho smiled and put his hands together as a sign of prayer. You see, prayer is everything. Like I already said, prayer draws God's mercy and compassion. It unfolds the favor upon you and your love ones.

Yes, it did for me. It breaks through to the heavenly realm. Heaven hears and the answer is instantly given. Praying at all times indicates to God that you want to be part of His army that stands for Him. God will answer you and equip you even when you don't expect it.

## WHY WE WATCH AND PRAY

We have looked into prayer in an expanded the concept. So, the next discussion should be why do we pray at all seasons and at all times?

Jesus said to His disciples pray so that you should not enter into temptation. Temptation simply means a desire to do something wrong or unwise. Jesus faced various forms of temptation when He was on the earth. One simple word that averts temptation is the word of God, "It is written."

Judas was one of Jesus' disciples but temptation pulled him down and he fall into the temptation of betraying Jesus Christ.

Jesus knew the temptation that would be coming to Peter, about the betrayal and needed to be praying for Peter. Luke 22:32

Jesus knew the temptation that will be coming on you, too, even though Jesus prayed for you according to John Chapter 17, He wants you to make prayer a lifestyle to avoid temptation.

Prayer gets us through everything. The tempter's focus is to make the child of God do many things that aren't related to God. To be disobedient to God's commandments is Satan's goal, but when we pray those plans will be averted. So, beloved people, make prayer a lifestyle event.

www.ingramcontent.com/pod-product-compliance
Lightning Source LLC
Chambersburg PA
CBHW021631120626
46545CB00002B/495